Charles King

Kitty's Conquest

Charles King

Kitty's Conquest

ISBN/EAN: 9783743305885

Manufactured in Europe, USA, Canada, Australia, Japa

Cover: Foto ©ninafisch / pixelio.de

Manufactured and distributed by brebook publishing software (www.brebook.com)

Charles King

Kitty's Conquest

KITTY'S CONQUEST.

BY

CHARLES KING, U.S.A.,

AUTHOR OF "THE COLONEL'S DAUGHTER."

PHILADELPHIA:
J. B. LIPPINCOTT COMPANY.
1890.

Copyright, 1884, by J. B. LIPPINCOTT & Co.

PREFACE.

The incidents of this little story occurred some twelve years ago, and it was then that the story was mainly written.

If it meet with half the kindness bestowed upon his later work it will more than fulfil the hopes of

THE AUTHOR.

February, 1884.

KITTY'S CONQUEST.

CHAPTER I.

It was just after Christmas, and discontentedly enough I had left my cosy surroundings in New Orleans, to take a business-trip through the counties on the border-line between Tennessee and northern Mississippi and Alabama. One sunny afternoon I found myself on the "freight and passenger" of what was termed "The Great Southern Mail Route." We had been trundling slowly, sleepily along ever since the conductor's "all aboard!" after dinner; had met the Mobile Express at Corinth when the shadows were already lengthening upon the ruddy, barren-looking landscape, and now, with Iuka just before us, and the warning whistle of the engine shrieking in our ears with a discordant pertinacity attained only on our Southern railroads, I took a last glance at the sun just disappearing behind the distant forest in our wake, drew the last breath of life from my cigar, and then, taking advantage of the halt at the station, strolled back from the dinginess of the smoking-car to more comfortable quarters in the rear.

There were only three passenger-cars on the train, and, judging from the scarcity of occupants, one would have been enough. Elbowing my way through the gaping, lazy swarms of unsavory black humanity on the platform, and the equally repulsive-looking knots of "poor white trash," the invariable features of every country stopping-place south of Mason and Dixon, I reached the last car, and entering, chose one of a dozen empty seats, and took a listless look at my fellow-passengers,—six in all,—and of them, two only worth a second glance.

One, a young, perhaps very young, lady, so girlish, *petite*, and pretty she looked even after the long day's ride in a sooty car. Her seat was some little distance from the one into which I had dropped, but that was because the other party to be depicted was installed within two of her, and, with that indefinable sense of repulsion which induces all travellers, strangers to one another, to get as far apart as possible on entering a car, I had put four seats 'twixt him and me,—and afterwards wished I hadn't.

It *was* rude to turn and stare at a young girl,—travelling alone, too, as she appeared to be. I did it involuntarily the first time, and found myself repeating the performance again and again, simply because I couldn't help it,—she looked prettier and prettier every time.

A fair, oval, tiny face; a somewhat supercilious nose, and not-the-least-so mouth; a mouth, on the contrary, that even though its pretty lips were closed, gave one the intangible yet positive assurance of white and regular teeth; eyes whose color I could not see because their drooping lids were fringed with heavy curving lashes, but which subsequently turned out to be a soft, dark gray; and hair!—hair that made one instinctively gasp with admiration, and exclaim (mentally), "If it's *only* real!"—hair that rose in heavy golden masses above and around the diminutive ears, almost hiding them from view, and fell in braids (not braids either, because it *wasn't* braided) and rolls—only that sounds breakfasty—and masses again,—it must do for both,—heavy golden masses and rolls and waves and straggling offshoots and disorderly delightfulness all down the little lady's neck, and, landing in a lump on the back of the seat, seemed to come surging up to the top again, ready for another tumble.

It looked as though it hadn't been "fixed" since the day before, and yet as though it would be a shame to touch it; and was surmounted, "sat upon," one might say, by the jauntiest of little travelling hats of some dark material (don't expect a bachelor, and an elderly one at that, to be explicit on such a point), this in turn being topped by the pertest little mite of a feather sticking bolt upright from a labyrinth of beads, bows, and buckles at the side.

More of this divinity was not to be viewed from my post of observation, as all below the fragile white throat with its dainty collar and the handsome fur "boa," thrown loosely back on account of the warmth of the car, was undergoing complete occultation by the seats in front; yet enough was visible to impress one with a longing to become acquainted with the diminutive entirety, and to convey an idea of cultivation and refinement somewhat unexpected on that particular train, and in that utterly unlovely section of the country.

Naturally I wondered who she was; where she was going; how it happened that she, so young, so innocent, so be-petted and be-spoilt in appearance, should be journeying alone through the thinly settled counties of upper Mississippi. Had she been a "through" passenger, she would have taken the express, not this grimy, stop-at-every-shanty, slow-going old train on which we were creeping eastward.

In fact, the more I peeped, the more I marvelled; and I found myself almost unconsciously inaugurating a detective movement with a view to ascertaining her identity.

All this time mademoiselle was apparently serenely unconscious of my scrutiny and deeply absorbed in some object—a book, probably—in her lap. A stylish Russia-leather satchel was hanging among the hooks above her head,—evidently her property,—and those probably, too, were her initials in monogram, stamped in gilt upon the flap, too far off for my fading eyes to distinguish, yet tantalizingly near.

Now I'm a lawyer, and as such claim an indisputable right to exercise the otherwise feminine prerogative of yielding to curiosity. It's our business to be curious; not with the sordid views and mercenary intents of Templeton Jitt; but rather as Dickens's "Bar" was curious,—affably, apologetically, professionally curious. In fact, as "Bar" himself said, "we lawyers *are* curious," and take the same lively interest in the affairs of our fellow-men (and women) as maiden aunts are popularly believed to exercise in the case of a pretty niece with a dozen beaux, or a mother-in-law in the daily occupations of the happy husband of her eldest daughter. Why need I apologize further? I left my seat; zigzagged down the aisle; took a drink of water which I didn't want, and, returning, the long look at the monogram which I *did*.

There they were, two gracefully intertwining letters; a "C" and a "K." Now was it C. K. or K. C.? If C. K., what did it stand for?

I thought of all manner of names as I regained my seat; some pretty, some tragic, some commonplace, none satisfactory. Then I concluded to begin over; put the cart before the horse, and try K. C.

Now, it's ridiculous enough to confess to it, but Ku-Klux was the first thing I thought of; K. C. didn't stand for it at all, but Ku-Klux *would* force itself upon my imagination. Well, everything *was* Ku-Klux just then. Congress was full of them; so was the South;—Ku-Klux had brought me up there; in fact I had spent most of the afternoon in planning an elaborate line of defence for a poor devil whom I knew to be innocent, however blood-guilty might have been his associates. Ku-Klux had brought that lounging young cavalryman (the other victim reserved for description), who—confound him—had been the cause of my taking a metaphorical back seat and an actual front one on entering the car; but Ku-Klux couldn't have brought *her* there; and after all, what business had I bothering my tired brains over this young beauty? I was nothing to her, why should she be such a torment to me?

In twenty minutes we would be due at Sandbrook, and there I was to leave the train and jog across the country to the plantation of Judge Summers, an old friend of my father's and of mine, who had written me to visit him on my trip, that we might consult together over some intricate cases that of late had been occupying his attention in that vicinity. In fact, I was too elderly to devote so much thought and speculation to a damsel still in her teens, so I resolutely turned eyes and tried to turn thoughts to something else.

The lamps were being lighted, and the glare from the one overhead fell full upon my other victim, the cavalryman. I knew him to be such from the crossed sabres in gold upon his jaunty forage cap, and the heavy army cloak which was muffled cavalier-like over his shoulders, displaying to vivid advantage its gorgeous lining of canary color, yet completely concealing any interior garments his knightship might be pleased to wear.

Something in my contemplation of this young warrior amused me to that extent that I wondered he had escaped more than a casual glance before. Lolling back in his seat, with a huge pair of top boots spread out upon the cushion in front, he had the air, as the French say, of thorough self-appreciation and superiority; he was gazing dreamily up at the lamp overhead and whistling softly to himself, with what struck me forcibly as an affectation of utter nonchalance; what struck me still more forcibly was that he did not once look at the young beauty so close behind him; on the contrary, there was an evident attempt on his part to appear sublimely indifferent to her presence.

Now that's very unusual in a young man under the circumstances, isn't it? I had an idea that these Charles O'Malleys were heart-smashers; but this conduct hardly tallied with any of my preconceived notions on the subject of heart-smashing, and greatly did I marvel and conjecture as to the cause of this extraordinary divergence from the manners and customs of young men,—soldiers in particular, when, of a sudden, Mars arose, threw off his outer vestment, emerged as it were from a golden glory of yellow shelter-tent; discovered a form tall, slender, graceful, and erect, the whole clad in a natty shell-jacket and riding-breeches; stalked up to the stove in the front of the car; produced, filled, and lighted a smoke-begrimed little meerschaum; opened the door with a snap; let himself out with a bang; and disappeared into outer darkness.

Looking quickly around, I saw that the fair face of C. K. or K. C. was uplifted; furthermore, that there was an evident upward tendency on the part of the aforementioned supercilious nose, entirely out of proportion with the harmonious and combined movement of the other features; furthermore, that the general effect was that of maidenly displeasure; and, lastly, that the evident object of such divine wrath was, beyond all peradventure, the vanished knight of the sabre.

"Now, my lad," thought I, "what have you done to put your foot in it?"

Just then the door reopened, and in came, not Mars, but the conductor; and that functionary, proceeding direct to where she sat, thus addressed the pretty object of my late cogitations (I didn't listen, but I heard):

"It'll be all right, miss. I telegraphed the judge from Iuka, and reckon he'll be over with the carriage to meet you; but if he nor none of the folks ain't there, I'll see that you're looked after all right. Old Jake Biggs 'll be there, most like, and then you're sure of getting over to the judge's to-night anyhow."

Here I pricked up my ears. Beauty smilingly expressed her gratitude, and, in smiling, corroborated my theory about the teeth to the most satisfactory extent.

"The colonel," continued the conductor, who would evidently have been glad of any excuse to talk with her for hours, "the colonel, him and Mr. Peyton, went over to Holly Springs three days ago; but the smash-up on the Mississippi Central must have been the cause of their not getting to the junction in time to meet you. That's why I brought you along on this train; 'twasn't no use to wait for them there."

"Halloo!" thought I at this juncture, "here's my chance; he means Judge Summers by 'the judge's,' and 'the colonel' is Harrod Summers, of course, and Ned Peyton, that young reprobate who has been playing fast and loose among the marshals and sheriffs, is the Mr. Peyton he speaks of; and this must be some friend or relative of Miss Pauline's going to visit her. The gentlemen have been sent to meet her, and have been delayed by that accident. I'm in luck;" so up I jumped, elbowed the obliging conductor to one side; raised my hat, and introduced myself,—" Mr. Brandon, of New Orleans, an old friend of Judge Summers, on my way to visit him; delighted to be of any service; pray accept my escort," etc., etc.—all somewhat incoherent, but apparently satisfactory. Mademoiselle graciously acknowledged my offer; smilingly accepted my services; gave me a seat by her side; and we were soon busied in a pleasant chat about "Pauline," her cousin, and "Harrod," her other cousin and great admiration. Soon I learned that it was K. C., that K. C. was Kitty Carrington; that Kitty Carrington was Judge Summers's niece, and that Judge Summers's niece was going to visit Judge Summers's niece's uncle; that they had all spent the months of September and October together in the north when she first returned from abroad; that she had been visiting "Aunt Mary" in Louisville ever since, and that "Aunt Mary" had been with her abroad for ever so long, and was just as good and sweet as she could be. In fact, I was fast learning all my charming little companion's family history, and beginning to feel tolerably well acquainted with and immensely proud of her, when the door opened with a snap, closed with a bang, and, issuing from outer darkness, re-entered Mars.

Now, when Mars re-entered, he did so pretty much as I have seen his brother button-wearers march into their company quarters on inspection morning, with an air of determined ferocity and unsparing criticism; but when Mars caught sight of me, snugly ensconced beside the only belle on the train, the air suddenly gave place to an expression of astonishment. He dropped a gauntlet; picked it up; turned red; and then, with sudden resumption of lordly indifference, plumped himself down into his seat in as successful an attempt at expressing "Who cares?" without saying it, as I ever beheld.

Chancing to look at Miss Kitty, I immediately discovered that a little cloud had settled upon her fair brow, and detected the nose on another rise, so said I,—

"What's the matter? Our martial friend seems to have fallen under the ban of your displeasure," and then was compelled to smile at the vindictiveness of the reply:

"*He!* he has indeed! Why, he had the impertinence to speak to me before you came in; asked me if I was not the Miss Carrington expected at Judge Summers's; actually offered to escort me there, as the colonel had failed to meet me!"

"Indeed! Then I suppose I, too, am horribly at fault," said I, laughing, "for I've done pretty much the same thing?"

"Nonsense!" said Miss Kit. "Can't you understand? He's a Yankee,—a Yankee officer! You don't suppose I'd allow myself, a Southern girl whose home was burnt by Yankees and whose only brother fought all through the war against them,—you don't suppose I'd allow myself to accept any civility from a Yankee, do you?" and the bright eyes shot a vengeful glance at the dawdling form in front, and a terrific pout straightway settled upon her lips.

Amused, yet unwilling to offend, I merely smiled and said that it had not occurred to me; but immediately asked her how long before my entrance this had happened.

"Oh, about half an hour; he never made more than one attempt."

"What answer did you give him?"

"Answer!—why! I couldn't say much of anything, you know, but merely told him I wouldn't trouble him, and said it in such a way that he knew well enough what was meant. He took the hint quickly enough, and turned red as fire, and said very solemnly, 'I ask your pardon,' put on his cap and marched back to his seat." Here came a pretty little imitation of Mars raising his chin and squaring his shoulders as he walked off.

I smiled again, and then began to think it all over. Mars was a total stranger to me. I had never seen him before in my life, and, so long as we remained on an equal footing as strangers to the fair K. C., I had been disposed to indulge in a little of the usual jealousy of "military interference," and, from my exalted stand-point as a man of the world and at least ten years his senior in age, to look upon him as a boy with no other attractions than his buttons and a good figure; but Beauty's answer set me to thinking. I was a Yankee, too, only she didn't know it; if she had, perhaps Mars would have stood the better chance of the two. I, too, had borne arms against the Sunny South (as a valiant militiaman when the first call came in '61), and had only escaped wearing the uniform she detested from the fact that our regimental rig was gray, and my talents had never conspired to raise me above the rank of lance-corporal. I, too, had participated in the desecration of the "sacred soil" (digging in the hot sun at the first earthworks we threw up across the Long Bridge); in fact, if she only knew it, there was probably more reason, more real cause, for resentment against me, than against the handsome, huffy stripling two seats in front.

He was a "Yank," of course; but judging from the smooth, ruddy cheek, and the downiest of downy moustaches fringing his upper lip, had but just cut loose from the apron-strings of his maternal West Point. Why! he must have been at school when we of the old Seventh tramped down Broadway that April afternoon to the music of "Sky-rockets," half drowned in stentorian cheers. In fact, I began, in the few seconds it took me to consider this, to look upon Mars as rather an ill-used individual. Very probably he was stationed somewhere in the vicinity, for loud appeals had been made for regular cavalry ever since the year previous, when the Ku-Klux began their devilment in the neighborhood. Very probably he knew Judge Summers; visited at his plantation; had heard of Miss Kitty's coming, and was disposed to show her attention. Meeting her on the train alone and unescorted, he had done nothing more than was right in offering his services. He had simply acted as a gentleman, and been rebuffed. Ah, Miss Kitty, you must, indeed, be very young, thought I, and so asked,—

"Have you been long in the South since the war, Miss Carrington?"

"I? Oh, no! We lived in Kentucky before the war, and when it broke out mother took me abroad. I was a little bit of a girl then, and was put at school in Paris, but mother died very soon afterwards, and then auntie took charge of me. Why, I only left school last June!"

Poor little Kit! her father had died when she was a mere baby; her mother before the child had reached her tenth year; their beautiful old home in Kentucky had been sacked and burned during the war; and George, her only brother, after fighting for his "Lost Cause" until the last shot was fired at Appomattox, had gone abroad, married, and settled there. Much of the large fortune of their father still remained; and little Kit, now entering upon her eighteenth year, was the ward of Judge Summers, her mother's brother, and quite an heiress.

All this I learned, partly at the time, principally afterwards from the judge himself; but meantime there was the rebellious little fairy at my side with all the hatred and prejudice of ten years ago, little dreaming how matters had changed since the surrender of her beloved Lee, or imagining the quantity of oil that had been poured forth upon the troubled waters.

CHAPTER II.

The "Twenty minutes to Sandbrook" had become involved in difficulty. Interested in my chat with Kitty, I had failed to notice that we were stopping even longer than usual at some mysterious locality where there was even less of any apparent reason for stopping at all. All without was darkness. I pushed open the window, poked out my head, and took a survey. All was silence save the hissing of the engine way ahead, and one or two voices in excited conversation somewhere near the baggage-car and by the fence at the roadside. Two lights, lanterns apparently, were flitting rapidly about. I wondered at the delay, but could assign no cause in reply to the natural question Miss Kit asked as I drew in my head.

Mars opened his window as I closed mine, looked out a moment, then got up, gave himself a stretch, and stalked out; this time without slamming the door; a bang would have been too demonstrative in that oppressive silence. In one minute he came back with a quick, nervous step, picked up a belt and holster he had left at his seat, and, without a glance at us, turned sharply back to the door again. As he disappeared, I saw his hand working at the butt of the revolver swung at his hip. Something was wrong. I knew that the Ku-Klux had been up to mischief in that vicinity, and the thought flashed upon me that they were again at work. Looking around, I saw that three of our four fellow-passengers had disappeared. They were ill-favored specimens, for I remembered noticing them just before we stopped, and remarked that they were talking earnestly and in low tones together at the rear end of the car. The other passenger was an old lady, spectacled and rheumatic. Without communicating my suspicions to my little charge, I excused myself; stepped quietly out; swung off the car, and stumbled up the track toward the lights.

A group of six or eight men was gathered at the baggage-car. About the same number were searching along the fence, all talking excitedly. I hailed a brakeman and asked what was the matter.

"Ku-Klux, sir! Tried to rob the express! There was two of them in mask jumped in with their pistols and belted the agent over the head and laid him out; but afore they could get into the safe, the baggage-master, Jim Dalton, came in, and he yelled and went for 'em. We was running slow up grade, and they jumped off;

Jim and the conductor after them; that's why we stopped and backed down."

"Which way did they go?" I asked.

"Took right into the bush, I reckon. That lieutenant and another feller has gone in through here, and Bill here says he seen three other fellers light out from the back car,—the one you was in, sir. That's enough to catch them if they're on the trail."

"Catch them!" I exclaimed. "Those three men in our car were of the same gang, if anything, and that makes five to our four."

"Yes, by G—d!" said another of the party, a sturdy-looking planter; "and what's more, I believe they've got a ranch in hereabouts and belong to Hank Smith's gang. There ain't a meaner set of cut-throats in all Dixie."

"Then, for heaven's sake, let's go in and hunt up our party!" said I, really apprehensive as to their safety. Three or four volunteered at once. Over the fence we went, and on into the pitchy darkness beyond. Stumbling over logs and cracking sticks and leaves, squashing through mud-holes and marshy ground, we plunged ahead, until a minute or two brought us panting into a comparatively open space, and there we paused to listen. Up to this time I had heard not a sound from the pursuit, and hardly knew which way to turn. Each man held his breath and strained his ears.

Another minute and it came,—well on to the front,—a yell, a shot, another shot, and then,—"This way!" "This way!" "Here they are!" The rest was drowned by our own rush, as we once more plunged into the thicket and on towards the shouts. All of us were armed in one way or another,—it is rare enough that any man goes otherwise in that section of the country,—and to me there was a terrible excitement about the whole affair, and my heart came bounding up to my throat with every stride.

One or two more shots were heard, and on we kept until, just as every man was almost breathless and used up, we were brought to a sudden stop on the steep bank of a bayou that stretched far to either side of our path, right and left, completely barring farther progress.

In blank amazement, and utterly at a loss what to do, we were gazing stupidly in one another's faces, as one after another we gathered on the brink, when there came a sudden exclamation from the midst of us,—"Who's that?" I jumped, thanks to startled nerves, and looked around.

A dark form came creeping slowly up the bank, and a weak voice said,—

"Don't shoot, fellows. I'm all right, but they nigh onto finished me, and they've got Hank Smith away anyhow."

We crowded around him with questions; but

he was faint and sick and the blood was streaming from a cut on his forehead. A long pull at a flask tendered by some sympathetic soul in the group revived him enough to tell his experience.

"Me and the lieutenant took out through the open until we had to take to the bush. Didn't see the conductor nor Jim anywhere, but we gained on the Kluxers. Pretty soon we heard 'em busting through the bushes and heard 'em holler. I got blowed, but the lieutenant, he went ahead like as though he'd done nothing but jump since he was a pup. I never seen such a kangaroo. He got clean out of sight, and all of a sudden I heard him holler; and then came a couple o' shots; and pretty quick I came upon him and another cuss just more than going for one another in the bushes. The Yankee had him under, though, and had winged him on the run. When I came up he says to me, says he, 'You look out for this man now. He can't hurt you, but if he squirms, you put a hole in him. I'm going on after the others.' So on he went, and I took a look round. I'd sat down on the cuss to make sure I had him, and my pistol at his ear. He was lyin' right here a-glarin' up at me, and the moment I got a good, square look at his face, d—n my eyes if it wasn't Hank Smith! Then I began to feel bully; and just then I heard some other fellows running up, and thought it was our crowd, so I yelled out that I was here and had Hank Smith all right; and he kinder grinned; and they hollered 'bully' too; and next thing I knew one of 'em ran up and fetched me a wipe over the head and rolled me off down the bank, and there I've been mud-hugging ever since.

"I was stunned, but knew enough to lie quiet, and they got into some kind of a boat and went paddling off across the creek; but Hank was groaning and cussing so that I couldn't hear nothing but him. He swore by all that was holy that he'd have that Yank's heart's-blood before the month was out, and I tell you the lieutenant had better keep his eye peeled or he'll do it."

So we had lost him after all! It was too bad! and so said the conductor and baggage-master when they rejoined us a few minutes after, bringing with them the cavalryman, all three out of breath, covered with mud and scratches, and the latter looking very white and saying but little. I noticed that his handkerchief was bound tightly round his left hand, and divined the cause at once. My respect for Mars was rising every minute. He took a pull at the flask, looked revived, and as we all turned moodily back to the train, I asked him about his hurt. "Nothing but a clip on the hand," said he; "but I suppose it bled a good deal before I noticed it, and made me a little faint after the row was over. I suspected those fellows who were in our car; in fact, had been sent up to Corinth to look after one or two just such specimens, and was on my way back to my troop by this train. If that man *was* Hank Smith, as they seem to think, I would almost rather have lost my commission than him." Mars's teeth came together solidly as he gave vent to this sentiment, and his strides unconsciously lengthened so that I had to strike an amble to keep up.

By this time we had worked our way back into a comparatively open space again, and could see the dim lights of the train several hundred yards off. The rest of our little party kept crowding around us and offering my young hero cordial expressions of sympathy for his hurt, and, in homely phrase, many a compliment on his plucky fight. Mars took it all in a laughing sort of way, but was evidently too disgusted at the escape of his bird to care to talk much about anything. Nevertheless, before we got back to the train I gave him my name, and, as an old friend of Judge Summers's, whom I presumed he knew, trusted that I might meet him frequently, and that we might become better acquainted.

"Thank you, Mr. Brandon," he answered; "I have heard the judge speak of you, and am sorry I did not know sooner who you were. My name is Amory."

"Have you been long in the South?" I asked.

"No, sir; only a month or two. In fact,"—and here something like a blush stole up to the young fellow's cheek,—"I only graduated in this last class—'71—from the Academy, and so have seen but little of any kind of service."

"You're soldier all over, at any rate," thought I, as I looked at the erect, graceful figure beside me; and wondered—my thoughts suddenly reverting to Miss Kitty—how a young girl could find it in her heart to snub such a handsome fellow as that, Yank or no Yank.

A few strides more brought us to the train, where Amory, whose gallantry had already been noised abroad among the passengers, was immediately surrounded by an excited group of non-combatants, while I jumped into our car to see how my little *protégée* had fared during our absence. She looked vastly relieved at my reappearance, having of course learned the true state of affairs soon after our sudden departure. I told her briefly what had happened, taking rather a mischievous delight in dilating upon Mars's achievement, and affecting not to notice the expression of mingled contempt and incredulity that promptly appeared in her pretty face. Mars himself did not reappear: he had gone into the baggage-car to bathe his hand and accept the eager attentions of one or two Africans, native and to the manner born, who were vying with one another in brushing off the dirt from his snugly-fitting uniform. He was still surrounded by a knot of passengers and train-hands when I went forward to see how he was getting along, which I did when the train started, but we exchanged a cordial grip of the hand; and parted with the promise of meeting at "the judge's," or the cavalry camp, a few miles beyond, within the next two or three days.

The whistle for Sandbrook was just beginning as I rejoined Miss Kitty, and, after a vigorous life of at least two minutes, wound up in a dismal whine as we rolled in among the lights at the station. Yes, there they were, ready and waiting for us. The genial, gray-haired old judge and Miss Pauline herself, his only and devoted daughter, in whose arms Miss Kit was rapturously enfolded the instant she hopped from the platform. There, too, was old Jake Biggs, whom the conductor had mentioned as mademoiselle's escort in case no one else appeared,—Jake and his boon companion, his faithful old horse, "Bob," so named in honor of General Lee. Jake was an old colored servant of the Summers family, and had followed his "young massa," Harrod Summers, all through the war; had seen him rise from subaltern to colonel; had nursed him through wounds and illness; and at last when the war was over, and Harrod, who had gone forth with the enthusiasm and ardor of a boy, returned to his father's home, old Jake contentedly followed him, and settled down in one of the few log cabins that remained on the almost ruined estate of the Summers'. Jake was a "free nigger" now, but the world to him was wrapped up in old associations and "Marss' Harrod." No such soldier ever had lived as his "cunnel," no such statesman as the judge; no such belle as Missy Pauline. And Jake not only would not leave them, but in a vague and chivalric manner he stumbled about the premises, lording it over the young niggers and making mighty pretence at earning an independent livelihood for himself by "doin' chores" around the neighborhood, and in hauling loads from the depot to the different plantations within a few miles' radius of Sandbrook. He had managed to scrape up a dilapidated cart and harness somewhere or other, and poor old Bob furnished, greatly to his disgust, the draft and motive power. Having been a fine and spirited saddle-horse in his younger days, Bob had naturally rebelled at the idea of coming down to the level of the plantation mules, and had shown something of his former self in the vigorous and determined remonstrance which resulted on the occasion of Jake's first experiments with the harness; but beyond a temporary dislocation of buckles, straps, and dashboard, and a volley of African anathemas and "Whoa da's" from his master, poor old Bob's rebellion had accomplished nothing, and he had finally settled down into a resigned and dreamy existence, and went plodding about the vicinity with the asthmatic cart at his heels, a victim to the vicissitudes of war.

Jake was a pet of mine, and had amused me very much on the occasion of my first visit to the judge's, and that's why I tell so long a rigmarole about him. He stood there, a little aloof from the "quality folks," grinning and bowing, and making huge semicircular sweeps with his battered old hat, in his anxiety to do proper honor to the judge's guests.

I had a chance to receive my especial welcome while Miss Kit was being almost devoured by her relatives; and presently the baggage was all pitched off; the train moved on with a parting whoop; Mars appeared at the rear door and gave me a farewell wave of the hand; and then, leaving to Jake and Bob the responsible duty of transporting the young lady's trunks, we four—Miss Summers and Miss Kit, the judge and I—were duly ensconced in the comfortable old carriage, and went jolting off homeward.

Mr. Summers and I had much to talk about, and finding it impossible to get a word in edgewise with the two young ladies, who were fondling, fluttering, cooing, and chattering on the back seat in the most absorbed manner imaginable, we gradually drifted off into our law business and let them gossip away and exchange volleys of news and caresses.

The judge was deeply interested in my account of the adventure with the Ku-Klux, and much concerned about Amory's hurt.

I learned from him of the desperate and lawless character of the men who were generally believed to be the prominent members of the gang, and the perpetrators of the dastardly outrages that had been so recently inflicted both upon the negroes and the whites. The people were terrified beyond expression; several had been driven from the country; several had been shot down in cold blood. A defenceless girl who had been sent down from the North as teacher of the freedmen's school, had been dragged from her bed at midnight and brutally whipped by some cowardly ruffians. The sheriff, who had arrested one of the suspected parties, was threatened in an anonymous letter with death if he failed to release his prisoner within twenty-four hours. He called upon the citizens for assistance, but none was given, for the Union people were too few. A dozen men in mask surrounded his house the next night; his wife heard the strange noise, and went to the door; opened it, and was shot dead in her tracks. The jail was forced, the prisoner released and spirited off beyond the limits of the State.

All this was going on, when, to the great joy

of peace-loving people, and undisguised anger of the unreconstructed, a troop of United States cavalry came suddenly to the scene. Several arrests of known murderers and marauders were made; and, until that very evening, nothing more had been heard of the dreaded Ku-Klux. Indeed, it was by some persons believed that their organization was broken up, and nothing but the positive testimony of one of their own neighbors, the man to whom Amory had turned over his prisoner, would induce the citizens generally to believe that Hank Smith himself was concerned in the attempted robbery of the express car. The cavalry had been there just about a month when this affair took place.

CHAPTER III.

Miss Kitty's tongue had been far from idle all the time that the judge and I had been talking over these matters, but it was only just before we reached our destination that I heard her telling Miss Summers of the events of the evening. The moment she mentioned that our lieutenant was hurt, Miss Pauline started and exclaimed,—

"Oh, Kitty! You don't mean it! What *will* Major Vinton say?"

"Who is Major Vinton?" said Miss Kit.

"Major Vinton is the commanding officer of the cavalry, and Mr. Amory is one of his lieutenants. Father knows them both very well, and the major is with us almost every day," was the answer.

Miss Kit's eyes must have been as big as saucers when she heard that. I couldn't see, but knew it when she exclaimed, in tones almost horror-stricken,—

"Oh, Pauline! Do you mean to tell me that uncle and you receive Yankee officers! I wouldn't have believed it!"

"You don't know him, Kitty," was Miss Summers's quiet answer. "I believe that we owe father's life to him, and I know that, but for him, none of us could have remained here. He is a thorough gentleman, and you'd like him if you only knew him as we do. As for Mr. Amory, he is only a boy, to be sure; but the major says he is a fine officer, and I know that he is a real nice fellow."

Miss Kit relapsed into amazed silence; the judge added some few gentle words of reproof for her treatment of the youngster; and I was smiling to myself over the whole affair, when we drove up to the main entrance of their once beautiful home. A tall, soldierly-looking man opened the door, exchanged a word of greeting with Miss Summers as he assisted the ladies to alight, and then, as they scurried away up the stairs, I was introduced to Major Vinton.

Now, though we had never met before, the major's name was by no means unfamiliar. We were both New Yorkers; both had struggled through Columbia, and had many a wrestle with Anthon and Drisler; both had rushed to arms in heroic style and tramped off for Washington at the first call for troops. But I had speedily tramped back again; while he remained, chose the cavalry arm of the service, fought his way up to the command of his regiment; and when, in 1865, his services were no longer needed, sheathed his sabre: put aside his well-worn regimentals;

tried hard to interest himself in some civil pursuit; took a brief tour abroad, returned just as the new organization of the regular army was being made, and meeting one night a joyous bevy of his old comrades, regular and volunteer, with whom he had fought over every field from Bull Run to Five Forks, the old fire was fanned into a blaze, and in one week he found himself a successful candidate for a captaincy of cavalry. The "major" came afterwards "by brevet," and Vinton had settled down into contentedly following the old life, though in a less exciting time and exalted capacity. He greeted me in a frank, warm-hearted way; and we were in the midst of a comparison of notes as to old college names, when the judge interrupted us with,—

"Vinton, Mr. Brandon brings important news, which I think you ought to know at once." So once again the story of our little adventure was told.

The major listened attentively and never interposed a word; but his brow darkened and his face set when I came to Amory's wound and Hank Smith's parting threat. The instant I finished he turned to a servant, saying,—

"Be good enough to tell my orderly to bring the horses round at once."

In vain the judge begged him to stay and have supper, or at least some little refreshment. The major said, very quietly, that he must be off to camp at once; asked me one or two more questions in a business-like way; and the moment the horses came, bade us good night, swung into saddle, and followed by his orderly, disappeared at a rapid trot. The judge and I stood listening on the portico until the hoof-beats died away, and then returned to the blaze of the great wood-fire in the sitting-room. The young ladies came fluttering down-stairs. Supper was announced. Miss Pauline looked inquiringly around as we walked into the next room, where a bounteous table was spread.

"Where is Major Vinton, father?"

"Gone back to camp, dear. He asked me to present his excuses to you, but he was obliged to leave as soon as he heard of this affair."

I fancied that a shade of disappointment settled on Miss Summers's face, but she merely answered, "Indeed, I'm very sorry," and busied herself with the tea and coffee.

Miss Kit looked immensely relieved, and immediately became radiant;—chattered like a little magpie,—in fact, was as charming and bewitching as possible; but it was already late; good-nights were soon exchanged; and, tired out, the household went to sleep.

Next morning when we assembled in the breakfast-room, our little heroine looked fresher, prettier, and *tinier* than the day before. This time her hair was "fixed," and that was the only point that in my eyes was no improvement. All day long the judge and I roamed about the premises or pored over the cases he had on hand. All day long the young ladies laughed, chatted, flitted about from one room to another, played and sang. No news came from the camp. Late in the afternoon, when we were all standing on the portico, a solitary trooper came cantering up the road along which the major had disappeared the night before. Without knowing why, I found my eyes turning upon Miss Summers. She was listening abstractedly to Miss Kit's account of a visit to the Mammoth Cave, but *her* eyes were fixed upon the horseman as he rapidly neared the gate,—neared it, and, never drawing rein or checking speed, rode stolidly past on the road to Sandbrook depot. The wistful, almost eager light faded from her soft brown eyes; the full lip quivered one little bit; but quickly rallying, she plunged into a blithe wordy skirmish with her cousin about some alleged flirtation of the summer previous.

Evening came, and with it Harrod Summers and Mr. Peyton; both making much over Miss Kit; both bemoaning the accident which had prevented their meeting; and both apparently pleased to know that "Mr. Brandon was *so* kind and attentive." I had known Harrod slightly before, as he was away much of the time of my previous visit; but I knew him to be his father's son, a man to be honored and respected. Of Peyton, the less said the better. He was a rash, foolhardy, and, I feared, criminally reckless boy, a violent "reb" and unsparing hater of every Yankee. I had heard grave stories concerning his connection with some of the acts of violence committed upon the Union-loving people in the vicinity, and had noticed the troubled look on the judge's face every time his name was mentioned. I knew that he had been arrested, and that there was strong presumptive evidence as to his guilt; but he had been immediately bailed out and released. After this occurrence, the judge had managed to persuade him to take a trip to Havana and New Orleans; but the moment he heard of Miss Kitty's projected visit he came hurrying back. They were second cousins, and had met abroad. Rumor had it that Peyton had offered himself; that Miss Kit had a girlish fancy for him; that his suit promised favorably until Aunt Mary became suddenly aware of this nice little family arrangement, and, being a woman of the world, and possessed of a keen sense of what constituted the eligible and ineligible in a young man, swooped remorselessly down upon the blissful pair; hustled Master Ned into immediate exile; and, gathering her one chicken under the shadow of her protecting wing, bore her in triumph away to a realm uninfested with dangerous young men. Miss Kit is said to have shed bitter tears one week; sulked the next; pouted another; to have made a vigorous and romantic attempt at pining in all three; but the effort was too much for her; and, being wisely left to herself, it was not long before Peyton and his escapades were to her matters of serene indifference.

Not so with him, however. To do him justice, Peyton was probably very much in love; and at all events had a very correct idea of the unlimited benefits to be obtained through the medium of Miss Kit's solid bank account. He was no fool, if he was a reprobate; and was as handsome and naughty a wolf as could be found infesting Southern sheepfolds; and here he was, primed and ready to renew the attack. The judge didn't like it; Miss Summers didn't; nor Harrod; nor I; but it only took a few hours to convince us all that our beauty had just enough feminine mischief in her to enjoy the prospect of another flirtation with her old flame; and so to all but Peyton and to her, the evening passed gloomily enough. The judge retired to his library; Miss Summers played soft, sad music at the piano; and Harrod and I smoked cigar after cigar upon the porch.

Ten o'clock came and still the pair were cooing away in the corner; Kitty's low, sweet, bubbling laugh floating out through the open casement to where we sat. Miss Summers closed her piano abruptly; came out to our nook on the portico; and, declining the offer of a chair, stood leaning her hand upon her brother's shoulder.

Harrod looked fondly up at her for a moment or two as she gazed out towards the gate; then a teasing smile played about his mouth as he asked,—

"Anybody been here to-day, Paulie?"

"No-o-o-o! That is, nobody to speak of."

"No major, then?"

Pauline looks squarely down into her brother's eyes as she answers, "No major, if you refer to Major Vinton." A little heightened color, perhaps, but that's all. She is as brave as Harrod and not easy to tease.

Harrod turns to me: "Do you think he has gone after those men with his troop, Mr. Brandon?"

"I don't know, colonel; he said nothing about it, but rode off immediately. I shouldn't wonder, though; for the judge tells me he is over here almost every day."

"Ye-e-es?" (inquiringly.) "How is that, Paulie?"

Paulie has no reasons to allege; probably he wouldn't come if he didn't want to.

"True enough," Harrod suggests; "and still less unless he knew he was welcome. He is awfully proud, isn't he, Paulie?"

"Indeed, Harrod, I don't know; but he is welcome, and any man who has rendered us the service he has in protecting our father against the fury of that mob on court-day, ought to be welcome among us!"—Color rising and a perceptible tremor of the hand on Harrod's shoulder. He takes it gently and leans his cheek lovingly upon it as he looks up at the flushing face, whose dark eyes still gaze unflinchingly into his own.

"You are right enough, dear, and you know I agree with you. He *is* a noble fellow, Brandon, and I hope you'll meet and know him better. Father's decision against two or three Ku-Klux raised a terrible row here; and as he attempted to leave the court-house with one or two friends the mob hooted him; and even his long residence among these people would not have saved him. They call him traitor and Yankee now. Well, father tried to speak to them, but they wouldn't listen. A few more friends gathered round him; a blow was struck; and then the mob charged. Shooting ensued, of course, and two of their own men were badly wounded, while father and his party of six barred themselves in the court-house. Old Jake Biggs dashed out to camp, luckily meeting Major Vinton on the way, and in five minutes from the time the first shot was fired, and before those howling devils could break down the door, Vinton darted at a gallop into their midst,—not a soul with him but his orderly,— rode up to the door as though he were built of cast iron, and then turned squarely and confronted the whole mob. There's only one thing on earth these people are afraid of, Brandon: they don't care a fig for law, sheriffs, or marshals, but they would rather see the devil than the Federal uniform. And for ten minutes Vinton and his one man kept that mob at bay; and then young Amory with half the troop came tearing into town, and if the major hadn't checked them, would have gone through that crowd in ten seconds.

"The mob skulked off; but they hate father and the cavalry most bitterly, and would wreak their vengeance if they dared. I was away in Mobile at the time, and knew nothing about the affair until next day, when my sister's telegram came; but the sheriff never tires of telling how the major rode into that crowd; and how mad Mr. Amory was because Vinton stopped his charge."

"No wonder you all think so much of him, colonel," I answered. "He comes of a noble old race, and whether as enemy or friend you cannot fail to respect him; and I'm glad to see a cordial feeling springing up between our sections in this way. I would to God it were more general!"

"Ah, Brandon, it is not the soldiers, not the men who did the fighting, who are bitter now. Our enemies in the North are the men who sat at home wondering why your Army of the Potomac didn't move. Your enemies are those who never felt the shock of Northern arms. We would have had peace long ago could the soldiers have been allowed to make the terms."

And so we sat and talked, until the clocks throughout the house were chiming eleven, and then Miss Summers declared we must retire. The corner flirtation was broken up; Peyton and Miss Kit exchanging a lingering and inaudible good-night at the stairs. Harrod and I closed and bolted doors and windows. Peyton stuck his hands in his pockets and walked nervously up and down the hall buried in thought until we had finished our work; and then, on receiving Colonel Summers' somewhat cold intimation that it was time to go to bed, wished us a sulky "pleasant dreams," took his candle and disappeared.

Harrod waited until he was out of hearing and then said to me, "They are all out of the way now, Brandon, and I want to see you one moment. It is a hard thing to say of one's own kinsman, but Peyton can't be trusted in this matter. Here is a letter that was left for father at the post-office in town, but I have opened and withheld it, knowing that it would only cause him unnecessary trouble. I'm worried about it, and had hoped that Vinton would have come over to-day; we're safe enough with him and his men."

Saying this he handed me the letter. I had seen them before; Ku-Klux anonymous rascalities,—a huge, coarse, brown envelope, directed in a sprawling hand to the "Honerable Judge Summers," and embellished in red ink with numerous death's-heads, K. K.'s, and in the upper left-hand corner a flaming scroll, on which appeared in bold relief the words "Blood! Death! Liberty!" The whole affair was ludicrous enough in appearance, and, throwing it to one side, I read the inclosure. It began with the usual "Death to Traitors," and wound up, after one or two incoherent "whereases" and "therefores," by informing the judge that if he remained in that vicinity twenty-four hours longer "all the damned Yankees this side of hell couldn't save him," and intimating that the lives of the Federal officers upon whom he relied "weren't worth their weight in mud."

Harrod and I sat for some time talking over this elegant document, and decided that nothing should be said until we could see Major Vinton on the following day. The camp was six miles away, and on the outskirts of the county-seat where the court-house row had taken place; and Sandbrook was nearly as far in the opposite direction. He anticipated no danger for that night; but such had been the reckless nature of the Klan, that we agreed it best to be on the safe side and to look well to our arms; then we parted, each to his own room.

CHAPTER IV.

It was a clear, starlit night and very mild, almost warm, in fact; and having spent my Christmas but a few days before amid the orange groves and magnolias of Louisiana, I had prepared myself for something more wintry on the borders of Tennessee; but up to that time my overcoat had been insupportable.

The combined effects of half a dozen cigars and the conversation just concluded with Harrod Summers had banished all desire for sleep. In fact, if I must confess it, I was nervous and ill at ease. The room seemed close and stifling, so I opened both window and door to secure the full benefit of the cool night-air, and then proceeded to make myself comfortable. First pulling off my boots and insinuating my feet into an easy old pair of slippers, I took the boots to the door and deposited them noiselessly in the hall, where small Pomp, the "general utility" man of the household, could find and black them in the morning. A dim light was burning on a little table in the hall, and I noticed Mr. Peyton's boots at his door, the door next to mine, and on the same side of the hall. We were quartered in what was known as the east wing, a one-storied addition to the main building, containing four sleeping apartments for the use of the judge's guests; the floor, as is generally the case in these Southern houses, being elevated some eight or nine feet above the ground.

Peyton and I were the only occupants of the wing that night; the rooms of the rest of the household being in the main building. It occurred to me, therefore, that the hall lamp was unnecessary there; and so I crossed over, took it from its table, and was returning with it to my own room, when I heard a long, shrill, distant whistle. It came from the direction of the woods on the eastern side of the plantation, so far away, in fact, that save in the dead of night it probably would have failed to attract attention. Involuntarily I stopped short in my tracks, listening; and involuntarily, too, I looked at Peyton's door. It was closed, but the transom above it was open, and all was darkness within. No sound had come from his room before, and I supposed him asleep; and now, as if in corroboration of that supposition, he began to snore; rather a louder and more demonstrative snore than would have been natural from so sudden a start, I thought afterwards. Meantime, I stood still a minute and listened. The whistle died away, and there was no answer or repetition; the snoring continued; I moved on into my room; closed and bolted the door; put my lamp on the bureau; took out my revolver and carefully examined it; then turned down the light until nothing but a mere glimmer was left; crouched down by the open window, and looked out. The stillness was so intense that the ticking of my watch and the loud beating of my heart seemed insupportable. Leaning out from the casement, I could see that Peyton's window, too, was open, and that there was a little shed of some kind beneath it, whose roof reached up to within about five feet of the window-sill. Garden-tools were probably stored there, as I had noticed a few spades and a wheelbarrow during the day. Peyton was still snoring, though less loudly.

I listened for ten minutes more, and still no sound came from the direction in which I had heard the whistle, save the distant neigh of a horse and the occasional barking of dogs. Yet my nerves were upset. That whistle *must* have been a signal of some kind, and, if so, what did it portend? At last, being unable to arrive at any conclusion, I determined to lie down and think it over; and so, taking off coat and waistcoat, and putting on a loose wrapper, I threw myself upon the bed. It must have been after midnight then, yet I could not sleep, and at the same time thinking was an effort. I found myself listening intently for every sound, and holding my breath every time the distant bark of a dog or the lowing of cattle was heard.

An hour passed; nothing further happened; and I began to feel drowsy at last and to regard myself as the easiest man to scare in the whole county. Soon after, I must have fallen into a doze; an uneasy, fitful slumber it must have been, too; for the very next thing I knew I found myself sitting bolt upright; every nerve strained; and listening with beating heart to the same signal whistle; only this time, though low and cautious, it was nearer; and, unless I was vastly mistaken, came from a little clump of trees just beyond the eastern fence. Harrod's big Newfoundland, who always slept on the porch in front of the house, and seldom, if ever, barked or made any disturbance at night, came tearing around to our side, growling fiercely, and evidently excited and alarmed.

Something was up, that was certain; and immediately I began to wonder what ought to be done. The call was not repeated; all was soon quiet again. "Blondo" had given one or two low, short barks; scouted through the grounds about the house; and returned to the southern front again. After one or two moments' consideration he had given another, a sort of interrogatory bark, as though he expected a reply; and then, with a dissatisfied sniff at hearing nothing further, slowly returned to his usual post.

Blondo's nerves were better than mine. I thought over the matter ten minutes longer in the most undecided manner imaginable. Harrod had plainly intimated that he suspected Mr. Peyton of complicity with the Ku-Klux or I would have awakened him; as it was, I was possessed with the idea that he ought to know nothing of our suspicions, nothing of the anonymous letter (from us, at least), and in no manner or way be admitted to confidence. Rather hard on Peyton, to be sure; but there *was* something about him I didn't like, something besides the mere fact that I saw he didn't like me, and—— What was that! There *could* be no mistake! I plainly saw through my open window a sudden gleam of light among the leaves of the oak-tree on the other side of the garden-walk. It was as though the light had been momentarily thrown upon it from a bull's-eye lantern and instantly withdrawn. More than that, the light was thrown upon it from this side. Thoroughly aroused now, I stole noiselessly from the bed; took my revolver; and, making the least possible "creak" in turning the key, I slowly opened my door, and on tiptoe and in stocking feet crept out into the hall. My plan was to go and arouse Harrod.

Without closing my door I turned stealthily away; and, as a matter of course, stumbled over one of my boots. There they were, right at the door, just where I had left them, and visible enough for all practical purposes in the dim light that came from my open doorway and the window at the end of the hall. It was clumsy and stupid in me. I looked towards Peyton's door, wondering if the noise, slight as it was, had awakened him. No more snoring, at all events. I took a step or two towards his room to listen, looked carefully down to see that I didn't stumble over his boots too, and then stopped short.

Peyton's boots were no longer there.

For a moment I could not realize it; then I stole closer to the door, and the door that I knew was tightly closed when I came up-stairs was now unlatched and partly open. The conviction forced itself into my mind that my next-door neighbor was up to some of his old devilment, and that that signal whistle had some connection with the mysterious disappearance of his boots. Peeping through the partly-opened door, I could see the bed, its coverlet undisturbed, its pillows smooth and untouched. That was enough to embolden me, and at the same time make me mad. All that snoring was a counterfeit for *my* benefit, was it? I opened the door and looked in: no signs of its late occupant; Ned Peyton had gone.

Sorely puzzled what to do next, I sidled out again; sneaked out, I might as well say, for that's the way I felt; and leaving his door as I found it, returned to my own room and took post at the window. Curiously enough, the discovery of Peyton's absence and his probable connection with the mysterious signals without, had had a wonderful effect in restoring me to confidence and endowing me with a fabulous amount of pluck and courage. The idea of summoning Harrod was abandoned; the thing to be done now was to find out what my amiable next-door neighbor was up to; and, if possible, to do so without letting him know that his nice little game was detected.

A clock somewhere in the hall struck three while I was pondering over the matter. Ten minutes afterwards there came a stealthy step on the garden-walk, and the figure of a man emerged from behind an old arbor near the oak-tree. It was Peyton, of course, although the light was too uncertain to admit of my recognizing him until he came nearer.

I crouched down lower, but kept him in view. Cautiously and slowly Master Ned tiptoed it up to the little tool-house under his window; swung himself carefully up to the roof; crept on all-fours until he reached the top; and then, making very little noise, clambered into his window and disappeared from view. A moment or two after, I heard him softly deposit his boots in the hall; close and bolt his door; and soon after tumble into bed. Evidently, then, we had nothing further to fear for that night at least; and in fifteen minutes I was sound asleep.

At breakfast the next morning the household generally put in a late appearance. Peyton established himself at Miss Kitty's side and monopolized her in the most lover-like manner. Immediately afterwards the pair sallied forth for a walk. Miss Summers looked very anxiously after them until they disappeared in the shrubbery, and then turned to Harrod with an appealing look in her eyes.

"I don't know what to do, Harrod. I didn't imagine the possibility of his coming back here when we invited Kitty."

"Don't worry about it, Pauline. Mr. Brandon and I are going to drive over to the cavalry camp this morning, and this afternoon I'll have a talk with Ned. How soon can you get through your talk with father?" he suddenly asked, turning to me.

"Twenty minutes at most will be long enough," I answered; so he sent off to the stable to order the carriage.

The judge and I strolled slowly around the house, planning the course to be pursued in the prosecution of the men who had been arrested under the "enforcement act." As we sauntered along the garden-walk on the eastern side, I naturally glanced up at my window and Peyton's. A coarse brown envelope was lying right at the door of the little tool-house, the very place where he had clambered to the roof the night before. "We lawyers are curious," and, without interrupting the judge's conversation, I "obliqued" over to the left; picked up the envelope; dropped it carelessly into my pocket; and went on talking without having attracted the judge's attention to the movement.

After the judge had returned to his study, and before Harrod was ready, I had an opportunity of investigating this precious document. It only needed a glance to assure me that it was just such another envelope as the one which inclosed the Ku-Klux letter to the judge that Harrod had shown me, and that fact was sufficient to remove any scruples I might have had as to reading its contents. The envelope bore no mark or address. The inclosure was as follows:

"CAPTAIN PEYTON:

"DEAR SIR,—The Yankee major, with forty of his men, went off in a hurry late last night, leaving the lieutenant and about ten men in camp. They're after Hank and the crowd, but we got notice in time, broke up the ranch, and scattered. Hank's wound is pretty rough; he played a d—d fool trick in trying to get that express money, and the boys all think he'd been drinking again. Three of us took him over the Big Bear in Scantwell's boat, and on up to Chickasaw. He sent me back from there to see you and tell you to watch out for every chance to get word to him. He'll be at Eustice's, across the Tennessee, until his arm is well; and then he's coming back to get square with the Yank who shot him. The lieutenant has got an infernal bad cut on the left hand, and can't do nothing for the next week. Look out for signal any night about two o'clock. Burn this.

"Yours respectfully,
"BLACKEY."

Here was a pretty piece of villainy. I thought earnestly whether to show it immediately to Harrod and make a full *exposé* of Peyton's complicity with the affair; but, before I could decide, the carriage came; and with the driver listening to every word that was said, it was out of the question. It was scandalous enough as it stood without letting the servants know of it. We talked a good deal about their general performances, but in no way alluded to the latest developments of the Klan as we drove rapidly along. Neither expected to find Major Vinton there at camp; but I had reason to know that Amory would be on hand, and had determined to give him immediate information as to the whereabouts of Smith that he might send out a party to secure him.

Sure enough, only one or two soldiers were to

be seen when we drove up, but a corporal took us to Amory's tent. He sprang up from the little camp-bed in which he was lounging and reading; gave us a cordial welcome; and, in reply to our questions, stated that the major had gone out with three days' rations and nearly all the men, hoping to hunt up and capture the gang. A United States marshal was with him, who felt certain that he could guide him to the very point on the bayou where the fight had taken place. He had started about three o'clock on the previous morning, just as soon as rations could be cooked, and was determined to hunt them to their holes.

"I expect him back every hour, and am disgusted enough at being ordered to stay behind; but he and the doctor both forbade my going, so here I am playing the invalid." His arm was still in a sling and the hand closely bound.

We sat and chatted for some twenty minutes. Amory inquired after "the young ladies" very calmly; made no allusion to Miss Kitty's snub; accounted for his non-appearance the day before by saying that the doctor had insisted on his remaining quiet in his tent; and so neither Harrod nor I saw fit to make any apology for our troublesome little heroine. She was worrying all of us now,—innocently enough perhaps, but sorely for all that.

Harrod turned the subject to Hank Smith;

and, finding that Amory had not heard of his threat as related by the man whom his friends had "fetched a wipe over the head," repeated it to him, and warned him to be on his guard. Mars took it coolly enough; expressed his readiness to welcome Hank and his adherents to hospitable graves; and, except that his teeth came as solidly together as they had when alluding to the ruffian's escape two nights previous, displayed no symptoms of the slightest emotion at the prospect of losing a quart or two of "heart's-blood" within the month.

Presently Harrod drove off to the village to make some necessary purchases, promising to return for me within an hour. Then I lost not a moment in giving Mars my information about Hank Smith; where he was to be found, etc., but without mentioning Peyton's connection with the affair or stating how the news came into my possession. He asked, of course, but I gave a good reason for declining to name the person who had volunteered the news, at the same time assuring him of my belief in its truth.

Mars was all ablaze in a minute. Chickasaw was at least twelve miles away and to the north. Vinton's plan, and the marshal's, was to go southwest, should they find the ranch abandoned, and search a number of suspected points in Tishomingo and Prentiss Counties. All the gang by this time knew that there was a hunt going on, and, at the cry of "Yanks coming," had scattered in every direction. Smith thought himself safe across the Tennessee, and would probably have only one or two men with him. Amory was fairly excited this time anyhow, and in ten minutes had made up his mind; gave his orders to a non-commissioned officer, wrote a letter to Major Vinton, with instructions to deliver it immediately upon the return of the troop to camp, and before Harrod Summers' return, had vaulted lightly into saddle, waved me a laughing good-by, and trotted off at the head of a little squad of five dragoons,—all the men he could possibly take. I watched them till they disappeared from view on the road to the Tennessee and then sat me down to wait for Harrod.

The corporal who had shown us to Amory's tent was on "sick-report" he said, with chills and fever. He, with three or four others, remained in charge of camp, and I amused myself listening to their talk about their officers and the Ku-Klux. An old darky on a mule came in to sell chickens, and after him, a seedy-looking fellow on a shaggy pony,—he "didn't want nothing in particular, unless it was to know when the captain'd be back."

The corporal was non-committal,—didn't know. The seedy party shifted around in his saddle, and, after profuse expectoration, "reckoned that the lieutenant warn't much hurt nohow."

"Why so?" says the corporal.

"'Cause he's off so quick again."

"That don't prove anything," says the dragoon.

"Whar's he gone to?" says Seedy.

"Don't know."

"Ain't gone far, I reckon; didn't take no rations, did he?"

"Don't know."

"I kind of wondered *why* he took the north road *fur*, if he wanted to catch the captain, 'cause I knew *he* was out towards Guntown."

"*How* did you know?"

"Well, I heard so, that's all."

The corporal looks steadily at Seedy, and is apparently suspicious. Seedy turns his quid over with his tongue and looks all around. He's a bad hand at extracting information, at all events. At last he makes another venture.

"Wish I knew how far up the north road the lieutenant went. I've got some business up towards the Tennessee. I belong to a missionary society hereabouts, and yet I don't like to take that long ride alone."

I hear the corporal mutter a rather unflattering comment on *that* statement; and it occurs to me that there is more of the odor of bad whiskey than sanctity about the member of the missionary society. He reminds me of Mr. Stiggins; and Mr. Stiggins makes one more attempt.

"Whar am I most like to catch the boys by dinner-time?"

"Don't know."

The member looks incredulous and indignant; and after a long survey of every object in range about the camp, turns his dejected steed slowly around and shambles off, with the parting shot,—

"Reckon you never *did* know nothin', did you?" To which the corporal responds,—

"No; and if I *did*, I wouldn't tell you, Johnny."

Stiggins strikes a canter on reaching the main road, and disappears on the trail of the cavalry. Presently Harrod returns, greatly surprised at Amory's sudden expedition, and curious as to the source from which he derives his information. I hardly know what to say, but finally get out of it by the explanation that it was all "confidential," and that I could say nothing on the subject until his return.

On the drive home we come suddenly upon the troop itself, looking tired and dusty, but returning from the two days' trip to Tishomingo partially successful, and with six rough-looking specimens of "corn-crackers" footing it along between the horsemen. They found no trace of Smith, the marshal tells us, as the men go filing by; but, after all, their luck has been good, and six of the worst characters are now securely under guard.

The major, he tells us, had stopped at Judge Summers's, and expected to find us there; so we whip up and hurry on.

A brisk drive brings us to the plantation in a very few minutes. As we rattle up to the doorway, Harrod catches sight of Mr. Peyton lounging on the portico by the open window of the parlor, for once in his life paying little or no attention to Miss Kitty, who is seated on the old wicker-work sofa, some distance from him, pouting and puzzled.

Harrod warns me to say not a word of Lieutenant Amory's expedition until Peyton is out of the way. Old Jake detains him a moment about "dis yer Hicks's mule done broke into the *gyarden* las' night," and I move on into the house.

In the parlor are the judge, Major Vinton, and Pauline; the first listening, the second narrating, the third as complete a contrast to Miss Kit as can be imagined. Vinton rises and greets me. He looks dusty, tanned, and travel-stained, but more soldierly than ever in his dark-blue jacket and heavy boots. After Harrod's entrance he resumes his story,—he was telling of the capture of the Ku-Klux,—talking frankly and as though none but friends were near. Harrod shifts uneasily in his chair and glances nervously towards the window. Peyton is invisible, but, beyond doubt, there, and a listener.

It is vain to attempt to warn the major; by

this time Peyton knows the whole story, knows who had aided the troops in their search, knows just how the evidence was procured which led to the arrest of the six victims, and doubtless his black-list is swelled by the addition of several names destined to become the recipients of Ku-Klux attentions.

Lunch is announced, and we all sit down at the table, Peyton and Kit coming in from the porch and endeavoring to ignore Major Vinton, a circumstance which apparently renders him no uneasiness whatever. He talks constantly with Pauline, and never gives a glance at the pair. Harrod and I are nervous. I watch Peyton closely, and it requires no penetration to see that not a word of Vinton's is lost on him.

Suddenly there comes the clatter of hoofs on the ground without; the clank of a cavalry sabre, and, a moment after, the ring of spurred heels along the hall. A servant announces the major's orderly; and, begging the major not to rise, the judge directs that the trooper be shown in.

Just as I thought, it is Amory's letter.

"Sergeant Malone said that it was to be given the major directly he returned. Them was the loot'nant's orders, and he told me to ride right over with it, sir," says the orderly. And, apologizing to Miss Summers, the major opens it and begins to read.

I glance at Harrod; his eyes are fixed on

Peyton; Peyton's furtively watching Vinton. Another minute and Vinton has risen to his feet; an eager, flashing light in his eyes, but his voice steady and calm as ever, as he says,—

"Gallop back. Tell Sergeant Malone to send me a dozen men, armed and mounted at once, and you bring my other horse." Away goes the orderly, and then in reply to the wistful look of inquiry in Pauline's eyes, the major says,—

"I must be off again. Amory has obtained information as to the whereabouts of Smith and some of his gang, and has started after them, but with only five men, too few to cope with such desperadoes. He has four hours the start of me now, and 'twill be nearly five before my men can get here; but I must reach him before he attempts to recross the Tennessee."

I cannot be mistaken in Peyton's start of astonishment. Instantly his face turns pale; the secret is out, his complicity perhaps detected. Lunch is forgotten, and we all rise and leave the table. Harrod manages to whisper a caution to the major to say nothing more while Peyton is near, whereat Vinton looks vacant and aghast. Five minutes more and Peyton and Kitty are missed,—gone out for a walk, the servant says. Then Harrod explains, and Vinton looks as though biting his own tongue off close to the roots would be the most congenial and exhilarating recreation that could be suggested. He is annoyed beyond expression, but it is too late now. Peyton is off; no one knows which way, and in half an hour all the real or supposable Ku-Klux in the county will know of the danger that threatens them; know, too, how small a force young Amory has taken with him in his hurried raid to the Tennessee; and, ten to one, if he succeed in capturing Smith, he cannot attempt to recross the river without having to fight his way through.

All this is canvassed in the anxious council that ensues. No time is to be lost; he must be reinforced at once. Harrod orders out his two horses; old Jake is hastily summoned and told to bring up his charger, "Bob"; and while the horses are being saddled, Vinton decides on his plan. He and Harrod are to gallop on after Amory; old Jake to ride down to meet the troopers, with orders to make all speed possible to the Tennessee. I am possessed with an immediate thirst for human gore, and want to go with the major; but there is no other horse, and I couldn't ride without shaking myself to pieces and capsizing every hundred yards or so if there were. To me, therefore, is assigned the cheerful duty of remaining at the plantation and watching Peyton's movements should he return.

Just before the horses are brought around, Kitty comes back, alone. She looks white and scared, and hurries up the steps as though anxious to avoid us, but Harrod intercepts and leads her to one side. She grows paler as he questions and talks to her; and suddenly bursts into tears, and rushes past him into the house.

"He's gone, by heaven!" says Harrod, as he rejoins us. "Kitty says he took the overseer's horse and galloped off towards the north."

"Here, Jake," says Vinton, "waste no time now; ride as though the devil chased you. Tell Sergeant Malone to follow as fast as he can. Don't spare the horses!"

Jake makes a spring; lights on his stomach on old "Bob's" withers; swings himself round; and barely waiting to get his seat, makes vigorous play with both heels on his pet's astonished ribs, and with a "Yoop, da!" our Ethiopian aide-de-camp clatters away. Then comes a hurried and anxious leave-taking with Pauline and the judge, and in another minute our two soldiers trot out to the road. We watch the gallant forms till the riders disappear, and then turn silently away. Pauline's eyes are dim with tears, and she seeks her own room.

That was a wretched afternoon and evening. Kitty never appeared. Pauline came down to tea and tried to entertain me during the long hours that dragged slowly away; but we started at every sound, and when midnight came she retired altogether. We had hoped for news, but none reached us.

The judge dozed fitfully in his easy-chair, but I was too much excited to feel the least drowsiness; so, cigar in mouth, I strolled out to the gate and gazed longingly up the dim, shadowy vista through the woods where lay the road to the Tennessee along which our first news, good or bad, must come.

Two o'clock came first, and I was then reading, in a distracted style, in the library. The clocks had barely ceased striking when my eager ears caught the sound of hoof-beats rapidly nearing us. Down went the book; and in a minute I was at the gate, just in time to meet the horseman, a corporal of Vinton's troop.

"We've got the Ku-Klux all right, sir," he says, as he reins in his jaded steed, "but we had to fight half the county. The lieutenant's wounded, and so is Monahan, one of the men, sir. They are bringing them here, and I'm to ride right on for the doctor."

Off he goes before I can ask more. Pauline meets me as I return to the hall. She is pale as death and her whole frame shakes as she says, "Tell me everything, Mr. Brandon."

"Harrod and Vinton are safe; Amory and one of his men are hurt, and they are bringing them here," I answer.

She saw by my face that there had been a fight. What her woman's heart craved, was to know that those she loved were safe, unhurt, and returning to her. Then the next minute she is all sympathy, all tenderness, even, for our boy *sabreur;* and she occupies herself with preparations for his reception and nursing.

While we are talking, who should come noiselessly down the stairs but Kitty, dressed in a loose blue wrapper; her lovely hair falling down her back and thrown from her temples and forehead, her eyes red with weeping. Pauline's heart is full, and the sight of this sorrowing little object is too much for her; she opens her arms and takes her to her heart, and Kitty's sobs break out afresh.

"I *know* that something has happened," she cries; "*do* tell me. You all think I care for Ned Peyton, but I *don't*—I *don't!* And he was frightful to-day, and—and—if he did what he said he was going to do I'll never speak to him again."

Pauline tries to comfort and soothe her, but I want to know what Peyton's threat was; and have the unblushing hard-heartedness to ask.

"He declared that he would raise forty men and kill every man Lieutenant Amory had with him. He frightened me so that I did not know what to do. Oh, Paulie, *what* has happened?"

"We don't know yet, Kitty. Harrod is bringing Mr. Amory here. He was wounded, and there has been a fight, but we hope it was not serious."

Poor little Kit starts back in horror, and then

sobs harder than ever. It is impossible to comfort the child. She is possessed with the idea that in some way or other she has been instrumental in bringing the affair about. She is terrified at learning the part Peyton has played, and bitterly reproaches herself for the uneasiness her flirtation had caused us all. She is the most abject little penitent I ever saw, and her distress is something overpowering to a susceptible old bachelor. In the course of an hour she is persuaded to return to her room, but not without the interchange of multitudinous embraces and kisses,—Pauline, of course, being the party of the second part.

It is nearly daybreak when Harrod arrives, convoying a rusty old carriage which he has obtained somewhere along the Tennessee; and from this our young soldier is tenderly lifted by two of his troop and carried to the room opposite mine in the wing. Poor fellow! it is hard to recognize in the pallid, blood-stained, senseless form the gallant young officer of the night on the train.

While the doctor was examining his hurts and dressing the wounds, Harrod gave me a hurried account of what had happened. Amory had reached the Tennessee about two in the afternoon, and, leaving his horses on the south bank in charge of one man, crossed quickly and completely took "Eustice's" with its precious garrison of desperadoes by surprise. Luckily, Smith had but two of his gang with him. They hardly had time to think of resistance. Hank was found stretched out in bed and swearing cheerfully over the unexpected turn of affairs, but had sense enough to acknowledge that his Yankee adversary "had the drop on him," and surrendered at discretion. Securing him and his two chums, but leaving the other inmates of "Eustice's" unmolested, Amory in less than an hour and a half landed his party once more on the south bank, and, after procuring food for his men and horses and resting another hour, started on the back-track about five in the evening; moving slowly, as his horses were jaded and his three prisoners had to foot it.

Their road was bordered by thick woods, and ran through an almost uninhabited tract. Hank was suffering apparently a great deal of pain from the fever of his wound, and, after sullenly plodding along about a mile, began showing signs of great distress. He was offered a horse, but declared that riding would hurt him just as much, and finally stopped short, swearing that "Ef you un's expects to git me to yer d—d camp this yer night you've got to do a heap of toting." Finding that he was really weak and sick, Amory was too soft-hearted to insist; and so a brief halt was ordered while one of the men went in search of a farm-wagon. Just at night-fall a horseman came cantering rapidly up the road, at sight of whom the prisoners exchanged quick, eager glances of intelligence, and attempted to spring to their feet and attract his attention. No sooner, however, had he espied the party than he stopped short; reined his horse about; and, digging spur into him, disappeared at a gallop into the shadows of the forest.

The whole thing was so sudden that no pursuit was made. Ten minutes after, there came the distant sound of a shrill, prolonged whistle, and Amory, thoroughly aroused, ordered a mount and immediate start.

Strange to say, Hank moved on with great alacrity. No man ever rose from so brief a rest so thoroughly invigorated. Once or twice more the same whistle was heard, but nothing could be seen, as darkness had set in.

Silently and anxiously the little party moved on, Amory riding several yards in advance, peering cautiously about and listening eagerly to every sound. All of a sudden from thick darkness came blinding flashes,—the ringing reports of musketry and pistols, and the regular old-time rebel yell.

Amory reeled. His horse reared wildly, and then, with a snort of terror, plunged down the road; his rider dragging over his side.

Of the next five minutes, none of the men could give a collected account. The sergeant had done his duty well, however; had kept his men together; and, what with superior discipline and the rapid fire from their magazine carbines, his little party proved too plucky for their assailants. There was a sound of scrambling and scattering among the shrubbery and of clambering over the rail-fence by the roadside. The fire suddenly ceased and the troopers were masters of the situation. During the excitement, one of the prisoners had managed to crawl off; while Hank and the other specimen adopted the tactics of throwing themselves flat on their faces. The soldiers were eager to pursue and capture some of the band; but the sergeant was wary and cautious; kept them on the defensive; secured his two remaining prisoners; and was just about ordering a search for their lieutenant, when the well-known and welcome voice of the major was heard down the road, and in a moment he and Harrod dashed up to the spot. Then came eager inquiries and the search for Amory; and presently a cry from one of the men announced that he was found. Hurrying to the spot, they discovered him, bleeding, bruised, and senseless, by the roadside; one deep gash was cut on his forehead, from which the blood was oozing rapidly; a bullet-hole and a little red streak in the shoulder of his jacket told where one at least of the ambuscading villains had made his mark; while the moan of pain that followed when they strove tenderly to raise him from the ground proved that our boy was suffering from still other injuries; but for all that, thank God! alive, perhaps safe.

It was long before the men could find a farmhouse; longer still before they came in with the lumbering old rattletrap of a carriage which their major had directed them to secure at any cost; and all this time poor Amory lay with his head on Vinton's lap, utterly unconscious of the latter's grief, of his almost womanly tenderness; but at last they were able to lift him into the improvised ambulance; and while the troopers, now reinforced by the small party which had followed Vinton, took charge of the prisoners, with orders to turn them over to the marshal at Sandbrook, the others drove carefully and slowly homewards, and so once more Mars was in our midst,—now our pet and hero.

All night long we watched him. All next day he tossed in feverish delirium; and when night came, Vinton and Pauline were bending over him striving to soothe and calm the boy in his restless pain. He spoke but little. Muttered words, half-broken sentences, incoherent all of them, were the only things we could win from him. He knew none of us; though he appeared to recognize Vinton's voice better than any. At last, late in the evening, when the doctor had forced an anodyne between his set teeth, Amory's muscles relaxed, he threw his unwounded arm wearily over his face and murmured, "I give up,—I'm whipped."

Vinton could hardly help smiling. "He thinks himself in one of his old cadet fights," said he. "Those fellows at West Point settle all difficulties with their fists, and this youngster was eternally in some row or other; he'd fight the biggest man in the corps on the slightest provocation."

We were all wearied with watching, and it was a glad sight when our pugilistic patient dropped off into a deep sleep. Vinton had to go back to camp to look after his men. Harrod was tired out and had sought his room. I had agreed to sit by Amory's bedside until midnight, as they had expelled me from the sick-room and made me sleep all morning "on account of age." Pauline was just giving a smoothing touch to the pillows when the door softly opened and who should come in but Kitty.

Yes, Kitty, our rampant little rebel Kit, who but a few days before had seen fit to snub our wounded boy simply because he was a "Yank" and wore the uniform which Uncle Sam has condemned his men-at-arms to suffer in. But how changed was Kitty now! Once or twice during the day she had stolen to the door or waylaid Pauline in the halls, always with a white, tear-stained, anxious face and a wistful inquiry as to how Mr. Amory was doing; then she would creep lonely and homesick back to her room; probably have a good long cry; and then down-stairs again for still another and later bulletin.

She had smoothed back her soft golden hair now; bathed away all but a few traces of the tears that had flown so copiously during the last thirty-six hours; and in her simple yet daintily-fitting dress, looked more womanly, more gentle and attractive, than I had ever seen her.

Walking quietly up to us, she put her little white hand on Pauline's shoulder, saying,—

"You go now, Paulie; it's my turn. You've all been working here and *must* be tired and sleepy. I'm going to play nurse now." And for a minute the corners of the pretty mouth twitch, and the soft gray eyes fill, as though our little heroine were again on the verge of a relapse into lamentation. Pauline's arm is round her in an instant, and she draws her close to her bosom as she says,—

"It is just like you, darling; I knew you would want to come." And then follows the invariable exchange of caresses so indispensable among tender-hearted young ladies on such occasions. Not that I disapprove of it. Oh, no! Only one can hardly expect to be "counted out" from all participation in such ceremonies and yet stand by and look on with unmoved and unenvying complacency.

Ten minutes more and Pauline has gone, with a good-night to both. The judge comes in and bends with almost fatherly interest over the sleeping boy; and as Kitty seats herself quietly by the bedside, goes round and kisses her, saying, "You are more like your dear mother to-night than I ever saw you."

Kit looks up in his face without a word, but in affection that is eloquent in itself. Then her little hand busies itself about the bandage on Amory's forehead, and my occupation is gone. Leaving her to attend to that, the judge and I seat ourselves at the open fireplace, waking and dozing alternately.

The doctor pronounced him better when he came next morning to dress the wounds. Mars spent most of the time in sleeping. Never did patient meet with care and attention more tender, more constant. Either Pauline or Kit was at his bedside. The old judge would come in with every hour or so. Vinton galloped over from camp and spent the afternoon; and as for myself, I was becoming vastly interested in helping Kitty, when, as bad luck would have it, old Jake brought me what he termed a "tallygraff" when he came back from Sandbrook late at evening with the mail; and the tallygraff sent me hurrying back to Holly Springs by first train the following day.

It was with no satisfaction whatever that I

bade them all adieu; though my heart lightened up when the doctor reported our "sub" improving. We all thought he recognized Vinton when the latter arrived in the morning to drive over with me.

We all thought, too, that a week at the utmost would bring me back with them in time to resume my functions as assistant nurse; but it was fully a month before my business could be completed, and by that time no further occasion existed for my services.

"We've had quite a little series of adventures, major," said I, as we whirled along towards the station, "and for one, *I* shouldn't be surprised if a spice of romance were to be thrown in; a love-affair, in fact. What do you think?"

Vinton knocked the ashes off his cigar on the dash-board; replaced his cigar between his teeth with great deliberation; smiled very quietly, not to say suggestively, to himself; gave a tug or two at his moustache, and then said,—

"Amory and Miss Kit you mean. Well,—I can't say. To tell the truth, I've been thinking for some time past that he has left his heart up North somewhere,—some old West Point affair, you know; writes long letters every now and then, and won't let me see the address; drops them in the postal-car himself, instead of sending them by the company mail; gets a dainty missive now and then, lady's handwriting, pretty monogram; and blushes, too, when I 'devil' him about Syracuse; they are postmarked from there. May not amount to much, of course. These youngsters get into that sentimental sort of vein at the Academy and seem to think it the correct thing to be spoony over somebody all the time."

That struck me as being a long speech for Vinton, a man of few words ordinarily. It occurred to me, too, that he was suspicious of his *own* affair's being the one to which I referred, and wanted to head me off. Oh, the perversity of human nature! *That* made me press the point and return to the subject. (Pauline afterwards said it was the meanest thing I ever did in my life. How little she knew me!)

"Don't dash my expectations in that way, Vinton. If Amory and Miss Kit don't carry out my plan and fall in love, I'll have to fall back upon you and Miss Pauline, you know; and just imagine how the judge and Harrod would feel at having to give her up. Besides, old fellow, you and I are cut out for confirmed old bachelors. Can't expect a young and attractive girl like her, who could marry anybody, to settle down to an *un*settled and nomadic existence in the army; that's altogether too much for so little, don't you see?"

"Job's comforters" would have proven a dead failure in comparison with that effort. It *was* mean, but there was something exhilarating about it for all that. What man, raised in a large family of sisters, doesn't grow up as I was raised,—a tease?

Vinton is too old a campaigner, however, and sees my game; grins expressively, and behaves with commendable nonchalance.

"I'll put the matter in train when I get back, Brandon, and try and arrange it between the young people to your satisfaction, so that you won't have to fall back on anything so utterly problematical as the other suggestion." That was all he had to say on the subject.

We reached Sandbrook; the train came; and in a moment more I was standing on the rear platform watching the tall, stalwart, soldierly form that waved me good-by, growing dim and dimmer in the distance.

That night found me at Holly Springs and in consultation with the United States marshal and the commanding officer of the little garrison of infantrymen. To the care of the last named, our captured Ku-Klux had been turned over, together with a few more of their fraternity, recent acquisitions, one of whom, the marshal informed me, was badly wounded and in hospital. He had been arrested the day after the ambuscade at a farm-house within five miles of the spot, and duly forwarded to join his Klan at their new and much anathematized rendezvous.

On my expressing a desire to see him, the

captain obligingly conducted me into the neat little hospital-tent, only a few steps from his own; and there, stretched out at full length, with a bandaged shoulder and a woe-begone countenance, was my missionary friend—Stiggins.

It was easy enough to conjecture how he came by his wound, though his own statement of the occurrence had surrounded him with a halo of martyrdom up to the time of my arrival. Stiggins had stoutly maintained that the Ku-Klux had shot him; that he was a law-abiding man, and that he hadn't seen a blue-coated soldier since the war. But when Stiggins caught sight of me he looked very much as though he had been lying, and in all human probability he had.

I said nothing to the officers on the subject until afterwards; when, in examining the articles which were in his possession at the time of his arrest, I came across a letter written in a hand I knew well enough, appointing a meeting with one J. Bostwick, and signed "Peyton." It was dated the night Harrod and Master Ned arrived at the plantation.

Stiggins swore he didn't know Peyton; never had seen him; "that note didn't belong to him nohow," and lied with a volubility and earnestness that would have done credit to a Jew in a clothing-store. But no information as to Peyton's whereabouts could be extracted from him or his unwounded confederates; nor could they be induced to give any clue which might lead to his implication. Whatever they were otherwise, they were game to the backbone; and stood by one another throughout their captivity and the trial which followed.

Hank Smith we found domiciled in the prison room where the gang were cooped up. He carried his arm in a sling, and a bed had been provided for his especial accommodation. He was surly and defiant, but accepted a piece of plug tobacco with much avidity, and was kind enough to say that " 'Twould be a derned sight better if you handed over a bottle of whiskey with it," which sentiment was unanimously concurred in by the assembled delegates, but vetoed by the captain.

Two weeks passed away, and still was I detained. Then came a summons to Jackson, where the State Legislature was in session. I had written to the judge and to Vinton. The former had been called South on business, but while at Jackson the latter's reply reached me,—a long, and for him, gossipy letter.

Amory was rapidly recovering, and the moment he was well enough to be moved—in fact, as soon as he had his ideas about him—had insisted on being carried to camp. It was in vain that Harrod, Pauline, and Vinton had protested; go he would. No persuasions could induce him to remain where he was a burden and a care to them. Kitty had taken no part in the discussion, and had been but little in the sick-room after he had recognized her; but the poor child was possessed with the idea that he was determined to go simply on her account, and was very miserable in consequence. As a last resort, Pauline, "for whom he has a warm affection," had communicated this fact to her intractable patient, and his pale face had flushed up for an instant and he was at a loss what to say, but finally protested that it had nothing to do with his determination. That evening he asked to see her, and, in an embarrassed but earnest way, thanked her for nursing him so kindly and carefully. "I'll never forget how good you—you all were to me, Miss Carrington." And from that time until the ambulance came for him, two days after, whenever she chanced to come to the room he was very gentle, and in his whole manner seemed anxious to show her that not an atom of resentment or annoyance remained. "Somehow or other there's something wrong," Vinton wrote. "I can't get her to look or talk like her old self; she won't cheer up, and whenever she is in the room both of them are nervous and embarrassed, and though Miss Summers and I have striven to get them into conversation when the doctor would let him talk, it's of no use." Oh, the subtlety of feminine influence! Fancy Vinton in the *rôle* of match-maker! And so Amory was back again among his men, rapidly improving, but still, as Vinton said, "something was wrong."

Nothing had been heard from or of Peyton except an order for his trunk and personal effects, brought to the colonel by a total stranger. It was conjectured, however, that the judge had gone to Mobile during his trip, and that his troublesome kinsman was to be shipped off to climes where Ku-Klux were unknown, and where his propensities for mischief would have no field for operation. No further complaints of outrages or disorders; everything was quiet and peaceful, and men and horses were having a good rest.

CHAPTER V.

ONE bright, beautiful evening late in February, it was my good fortune to find myself once more within "twenty minutes of Sandbrook"; this time on no hurried visit, but with the deliberate intention of accepting the cordial invitation of the judge and Harrod to spend a month with them. I was to make their home my headquarters while attending to the limited amount of law business that called me to that vicinity. I had heard several times from the plantation since Vinton's letter, and the very last news I had received was penned by Miss Pauline's own fair hand, telling me in a sweet, happy, womanly letter of what neither you, who have had patience enough to read this, nor I could be in the least degree surprised to learn,—her engagement to Major Vinton. The major himself, she wrote, had been summoned as a witness before a court-martial, and would be gone several days, but back in time to welcome me. Then came a page about Amory: "He has entirely recovered; that is to say, he is as strong and active as ever; but still—I don't know how to express it exactly—he is not the same man he was before that night. You know that the wound in his shoulder was a very slight one, and that his injuries were mainly shocks and bruises received by being thrown and dragged by his wounded horse. When he was well enough to drive about, the major used to bring him here frequently; and I really thought that he and Kitty were going to become great friends, for they wore off much of the old embarrassment and seemed to be getting along so nicely. Then he used to ride over and spend entire afternoons with us; and then, all of a sudden, he stopped coming; only visits us now when he *has* to; and is so changed, so constrained and moody that I don't know what to make of it. I really believe that Kitty was growing to like him ever so much; and she wonders, I know, at this sudden change. Even when he *does* come he avoids and barely looks at her."

It was strange; and I puzzled over it for some time. Matchmaking was hardly in my line of business, yet no spinster aunt could have taken more interest in the affair than myself. I was really anxious to get back to the plantation and see what could be made of it.

Harrod and the carriage were at the station to meet me, and a rapid drive in the cool night air soon brought us to the dear old house again; and there on the broad piazza, in the broad, cheerful stream of light from the hall, stood the judge, Vinton, and Pauline; and in a moment I had sprung from the carriage and was receiving their warm and charming welcome. Vinton was as happy in his quiet, undemonstrative way as man could be, and the fond, proud light in his dark eyes as he looked down at the graceful form leaning so trustfully upon his arm, was a sight that made me envious. Presently Kitty came down; but not the Kitty of old. Ah! little girl, what is it that has made those soft eyes so heavy, so sad? What has taken all the color from those round, velvety cheeks? What has become of the ringing, light-hearted laugh that came bubbling up from heart-springs that seemed inexhaustible in their freshness, their gladness? It is of no use to smile and chatter and prate about your pleasure at seeing this antiquarian again. It is of no use to toss your little head and look at me with something of the old coquettish light in your eyes. You can't deceive me, little Kit; you are changed, sadly changed. I, who have been away so long a time, can see what others only partially notice.

During the evening we all gathered in the parlor, talking over the events of my previous visit. Kitty had early tired of any share in the conversation, and sat silent and absent, taking little heed of what was said, though once or twice, when we were not speaking of Amory, she rallied for a moment and made an effort. She had taken a chair near the window, and was more than half the time gazing dreamily out towards the road. At last Vinton said he must get back to camp, bade us all good-night; his orderly came round with the horses, and Pauline went out to see him off, everybody else just at that particular moment finding something of extreme interest which detained him or her in the parlor.

It is odd how long it takes to say good-night under those circumstances. Fully fifteen minutes elapsed before the spurred boot-heels were heard going down the steps; then there was another slight detention,—cause, unknown; time, three minutes and a half,—and finally the clatter of hoofs as they rode off, twenty-seven minutes by the clock after the time when the major had announced that he must be off at once,—couldn't stay another minute.

When the hoof-beats had died away, Pauline came back to us radiant, lovely; and even that tease Harrod could not find it in his heart to say one word on the subject of the major's unaccountable display of unmilitary tardiness, though he looked vastly as though he would like to. Good-nights were exchanged, and soon after I found myself cosily ensconced in my old quarters in the wing.

About noon on the following day Mars trotted up the road, and, throwing his horse's rein over the gate-post, came "clinking" up the walk. His heels were decorated with a pair of huge

Mexican spurs, with little pendants of steel attached to the rowels in such a way as to cause a jingling with every movement. I had gone out on the piazza to meet him, and he quickened his pace and waved his cap with a cheery "How are you, Mr. Brandon?" the moment he caught sight of me. As he sprang up the steps I saw that he had at least lost none of his old activity; and though thinner and a trifle paler than when I first met him, it was not at first glance noticeable.

After the excitement of our meeting was over, however, and we were chatting over the Ku-Klux entertainments, I noticed how soon he became just the restless, absent, constrained fellow that Pauline had described. He changed color and started every time a footstep was heard in the hall; greeted Pauline warmly when she came down, and seemed to be more himself when talking with her, but even then his eyes wandered to the doorway. Something was wanting; and at last he made a vigorous effort and stammered an inquiry as to "Miss Carrington's" health.

"Kitty is pretty well, and will be down in a minute. She was writing to Aunt Mary when you came. If I were Kitty *I* wouldn't come down to see you at all, Mr. Frank Amory, for you've not been near us for the last ten days, and I presume we owe this call entirely to Mr. Brandon."

Poor fellow! he fidgets and looks woe-begone enough; tries hard to plead constant duties, no lack of inclination, etc., and just in the midst of it all, the rustle of skirts and the patter of quick, light footsteps is heard in the hall, and Frank Amory starts up with the flush deepening on his cheek and forehead, and stands facing the doorway as little Kit comes in,—comes in with a face that flushes deeply as his own, with eyes that are raised to his but for one brief second and then seek any other object but the young soldier before her, with a nervous, fluttering reply to his " Good-morning, Miss Carrington; I hope you're well?" and finally, as she subsides into an armchair by the window, with an air of mingled relief and apprehension that puzzles me inexpressibly. Amory, meantime, has resumed his seat (on his forage-cap this time), and plunged hastily into a description of a marvellous horse they have just concluded to purchase for officers' use. He must be a marvel; and it is astonishing what an amount of interest Frank takes in telling Pauline all about his performances. Kitty sits by the window listening, but saying not a word; and after this sort of thing has been kept up some twenty minutes Pauline excuses herself.

"Now don't go till I come back, Frank; I'll only be gone a few minutes." And with a glance at me that seems, as Mark Twain says, "perfectly luminous with meaning" to her, but which in my masculine stupidity I fail to comprehend until some minutes after, that young lady makes her exit. Then Mars turns upon me, utterly absorbed in the same horse, and with distracting volubility tells me the same rigmarole he told Pauline, every word of which I had heard. Then he asks questions about Hank Smith that he had asked three or four times already, and just as I'm beginning to wonder whether his accident had not resulted in permanent injury to his mental faculties a servant appears at the door.

"Miss Summers says will Mr. Brandon please come and help her a minute." And as Mr. Brandon obligingly rises to comply with her request, Amory springs up too, whips out his watch, and exclaims,—

"By Jove! how time flies! I told Vinton I'd be back for afternoon stables,—*must* be off! Good-by, Mr. Brandon; come over to camp and see us. Good-by, Miss Carrington; sorry I have to hurry." And out he goes; clatters down the steps and back to his horse; throws the reins over the animal's head, and vaults into his saddle; and then, with one wave of his hand, dashes off at a mad gallop.

I turned again into the house, and this is what I saw in the parlor. Kitty Carrington, all alone, standing there at the window gazing after

Amory as he disappeared down the road; her tiny white hands tightly clinching the window-sill; two great big tears just starting from each eye and trickling slowly, heavily down her cheeks; her dainty form quivering with emotion. Little by little I am beginning to suspect the truth in the matter, and, as I turn softly away without attracting her attention, mentally resolve to unearth the whole secret. Pretty business for a man of my years, you will say, but " we lawyers are curious."

N.B.—Pauline didn't want me at all. It was a ruse to get me away.

For the next three days matters went on in pretty much the same groove. Amory came over to dinner once and was utterly absurd,— handed Miss Kit to her chair, took his allotted place beside her; and hardly addressed one word to her through the entire repast, though he gabbled unceasingly to every one else. Just as soon as we could finish our cigars after dinner, and an adjournment was moved to the parlor, he declared he must be off; said he had a whole heap of commissary returns to make up before morning; and, with the briefest possible good-night to the ladies and the judge, away he went.

Pauline looked puzzled, Vinton amused, and Kitty—out of the window.

That night Mr. G. S. Brandon, who has already played too inquisitive a part in this little affair, resolved, before closing his eyes for a good, old-fashioned sleep, that he might as well be hanged for a sheep as a lamb, and pry still further; but he never dreamed how odd would be the solution.

CHAPTER VI.

THE next day Harrod Summers and I drove over to the cavalry camp to see Amory. It was a crisp, cheery morning, just enough wintry rime in earth and air and sky to make rapid motion a keen delight. As we neared the spot, the mellow notes of the trumpet came floating on the breeze, and as we rounded a bend in the road, we came in sight of the troop itself trotting across a broad open field. Mars was taking advantage of the glorious weather to brush up on company drill, and we had arrived just in time to see it.

It was a very pretty, stirring sight to my eyes; for the dash and spirit of the manœuvres were new to a man whose martial associations had been confined to the curbstones of Broadway, barring that blistering march from Annapolis to the railway, and the month of *fêted* soldiering at the capital and Camp Cameron in '61. Harrod gazed at it all with professional calm; occasionally giving some brief and altogether too technical explanation of evolutions that were beyond my comprehension. But the one thing which struck me most forcibly was that, though frequently trotting or galloping close to where we sat in the buggy, Mr. Frank Amory never took the faintest notice of us. His whole attention was given to his troop and the drill; and with flashing sabre and animated voice, he darted here and there on his big chestnut sorrel, shouting, exhorting, and on occasion excitedly swearing at some thick-headed trooper; but for all the notice he took of us we might as well have been back at home.

"Rather a cool reception," said I, "considering the youngster was so anxious we should come over."

"Why, that's all right," said Harrod. "It is a breach of military propriety to hold any kind of communication with lookers-on when a fellow's at drill or on parade."

And yet to my civilian notions this struck me as being uncivil. Less than a month afterwards I saw the same young fellow sit like a statue on his horse, and never give the faintest sign of recognition when the girl I knew he—well, that's anticipating—when a party of ladies were driven in carriages past his troop, so close to his horse's nose as to seriously discomfit that quadruped, and one of the young ladies was Miss Carrington. To my undisciplined faculties that sort of thing was incomprehensible. I looked on at the drill for a while, wondering how in the world those fellows could manage to keep their seats in the saddle without grabbing the pommel, when Harrod remarked that he believed he would go on into the village to attend to some business, and leave me at Amory's tent until he returned. Of course I could only assent; and in another moment I was landed in front of the tent which had become so fixed a picture "in my mind's eye" since the afternoon Mr. Stiggins rode in to inquire where the lieutenant and his people had gone. A darky boy officiously brushed off the seat of a camp-chair, saying that "Mos' like drill'd be over in ten minutes." So I sat me down under the canvas to wait.

Amory's tent was not luxurious. It was one of the simple variety known as the "wall" tent, so called probably because for three feet from the ground the sides are vertical and give more room than the "A" tents of the rank and file. A camp-cot occupied one side; a canvas-covered trunk stood at the head. Then on the other side of the tent was a rude field-desk, perched on four legs; the pigeon-holes crammed with portentous-looking blanks and papers, and the lid lowered to a horizontal. On this lay a square of blotting-paper, covered with ink-dabs and some stray papers, an ungainly inkstand, and one or two scattered pens and holders. A looking-glass about the size of one's face was swung on the front pole. A rude washstand was placed near the foot of the bed. A swinging pole, hung under the ridge-pole of the tent, constituted the wardrobe or clothes-closet of the occupant, and from this several garments were pendent. There was no tent floor; the bare ground was the carpet; and but for one little table the abode would have been rude in the extreme as the habitation of a civilized being. The table in question stood at the entrance of the tent, under the "fly" or awning spread in front. A couple of pipes with brier-root stems lay thereon, and a jar of tobacco. But in an easel-frame of soft velvet, a frame rich and handsome, conspicuously so in contrast with all the surroundings, was a photograph—cabinet-size—of a woman's face. It was not there on the occasion of my first visit, nor was the table. But there sat the picture, the first thing one would notice in entering the tent; and, having nothing else to do, I proceeded to examine it.

A sweet, placid, sorrow-worn face; eyes whose wrinkled lids spoke of age, but yet looked calmly, steadfastly into mine. Scanty hair, yet rippling over the brows and temples as though indicating that in years gone by the tresses had been full and luxuriant. Scanty hair, tinged with many a streak of gray, and carried back of the ears in a fashion suggestive of the days that long preceded the war,—the days when Jenny Lind entranced us all at Castle Garden (though I claim to have been but a boy then); when Mario and Grisi were teaching us Knickerbockers the beauties of Italian opera; when Count D'Orsay was the marvel of metropolitan society; when daguerreotypes were first introduced along Broadway. All these I thought of as I looked into this placid face, so refined in its every line; marking, too, that at the throat was clasped a portrait in plain gold frame, the inevitable indication that the wearer was of Southern birth, for none but our Southern women wear thus outwardly the portraits of those they love and have lost. The picture fascinated me; it was so sweet, so simple, so homelike; and, as I stood with it in my hands, I could plainly see the strong likeness between the features and those of my plucky young hero, whom I was half ready to be indignant with for ignoring me ten minutes before. His mother I knew it to be at a glance.

Just then came an orderly bearing a packet of letters. To my intense gratification—I don't know why—he saluted with his unoccupied hand as he said, "Letters for the lieutenant, sir." Was it possible that he thought I might be some staff-officer? He could not—that is, he would not, had he ever seen me straddle a horse—suppose me to be a cavalryman. Perhaps he had heard I was with the lieutenant the night he nabbed Hank Smith; perhaps he—why, perhaps they—the troop—had heard I had charged through the woods to his support. Well, I took with dignified calm the bundle of letters he handed me, and endeavored to look the suppositious character and place them carelessly on the table, when the superscription of the very first one attracted my attention. The writing was strangely familiar. There were four letters,—two "official," long and heavy; two personal, and evidently of feminine authorship. It was my business to lay them on the table. I did nothing of the kind. Holding the package in both hands, I sat stupidly staring at the topmost letter,—a tiny, dainty affair,—and striving to come back from dreamland. Where had I seen that superscription before? There stood the address, "Lieut. Frank Amory, —th U. S. Cavalry, Sandbrook Station, Memphis and Charleston R. R., Alabama," every letter as perfectly traced as through by the hand of an engraver; every i dotted, every t crossed, every capital having its due proportion, every letter wellnigh perfect. The superscription itself was a chirographic marvel. The writing was simply beautiful, and I had seen it before. It was familiar to me, or at least *had* been well known. Pondering over it, I gazed, of course, at the postmark: a mere blur. Something or some place in New York was all I could make out before it suddenly occurred to me that the whole thing was none of my business anyhow. I set the packet down on the table and strove to shut it from my mind; but there that letter lay on top, staring me in the face; I could not keep my eyes from it. I turned, picked it up and placed it on the desk inside the tent; dropped a handkerchief that was lying there over it; and returned to my place under the fly. I wanted to keep it out of my sight.

Presently, the bustle and laughter among the tents of the soldiers near me gave warning that the troop had come in from drill. The next moment, as I was again holding and looking at the picture in the velvet frame, Mars came springily forward, his sabre and spurs clinking with every stride. He pulled off his gauntlet, and held out his hand with a cheery and cordial "So glad to see you, Mr. Brandon," and then, as I was about to apologize for taking liberties with his belongings, he said,—and how can I throw into the words the tremulous tenderness of his voice?—

"That's mother. My birthday present. It only came a few days ago, and I like to have it out here with me."

And the boy took it from my hands, and stood for a moment, all glowing as he came from his rapid drill, and with the beads of perspiration on his face, and looked fondly at it.

"It's the only decent picture I ever had of her, and, somehow, it almost seems as though she were here now. That Ku-Klux business upset her completely, and the blessed little mother wants me to pull out and resign; but I can't do that."

"I have been admiring it for some time, Mr. Amory. The face attracted me at once, and it was easy to see the family resemblance. May I ask where your mother is living now?"

"In Boston now, but I think she longs to come South again. The North never seemed home to her. Father was in the old army. Perhaps Vinton has told you. He was killed at Fredericksburg, at the head of his brigade; and my uncle, mother's younger brother, died of wounds received in the same fight." Amory's voice faltered a little and his color brightened. "Of course they were on opposite sides," he added, in a lower tone.

I bowed silently. Nothing seemed the appropriate thing to say just then. Presently Amory went on:

"You see I'm about all she has left in the world,—her only son. And when husband and brother were both taken from her at one fell swoop, it made it hard to let me take up father's profession; but it was always his wish, and the only thing I'm fit for, I reckon."

"Do Yankees habitually say 'I reckon'?" I asked, by way of lightening up the rather solemn tone of the conversation.

Mars laughed. "Why," said he, "I'm more than half Southern; born in North Carolina, and spending much of my boyhood there at mother's old home. They used to call me 'reb' the whole time I was a cadet. It is a wonder I wasn't an out-and-out 'reb' too. All mother's people were, and they never have been reconciled to her for sticking to father and his side of the question. Poor little mother," he added, while the tears gathered in his eyes, " she *is* alone in the world if ever woman was, and I sometimes wonder if I ought not to yield to her wishes and go and be a clerk of some kind."

All the glow, all the life that possessed him as he came in fresh from the exercise of his drill seemed to have left Mars by this time. He was profoundly sad and depressed. That was plainly to be seen. Hoping to find something as a distraction to his gloomy reflections, I called his attention to the mail that had arrived during his absence. He moved negligently towards the desk, raised the handkerchief with weary indifference, and glanced at the packet underneath. Instantly his whole manner changed; the color sprang to his face; his eyes flamed, and a nervous thrill seemed to shoot through his frame. Paying no attention to the others, he had seized the dainty missive that so excited my curiosity, and with a hand that plainly shook tore it open, turned his back to me with the briefest " Excuse me one minute," and was speedily so absorbed in the letter that he never noticed me as I rose and strolled out to the front of the tent and the bright wintry sunshine beyond. The boy needed to be alone.

Fully fifteen minutes passed by before he rejoined me, coming out with a quick, nervous step, and a face that had grown white and almost old in that time. What *could* be wrong with him?

"Mr. Brandon, I beg your pardon for being so inhospitable. My letters were important, and —and rather a surprise, one of them. It is just about noon. May I offer you a toddy? It's the best I can do."

Mr. Brandon, to the scandal of his principles, decided that on this occasion he would accept the proffered refreshment. It seemed to be a relief to Mars. He bustled about, getting sugar and glasses and some fresh spring water; then speedily tendering me a goblet, produced a black bottle from his trunk.

"Shall I pour for you?" said he. "Say when." And in a moment the juice of the rye and other less harmful ingredients were mingled with the sweetened water.

"You will excuse me," said he. "I never touch it, except—well, that drink I took the night on the train after our tussle with Smith is the only one I've taken since I joined the troop. I promised mother, Mr. Brandon."

The reader has already discovered that Mr. Brandon could readily make a sentimental idiot of himself on slight provocation. Hearing these words of Mr. Amory's and the renewed allusion to the mother who filled so big a place in the boy's heart, Mr. Brandon deposited his glass on the table and held out his hand; took that of the surprised young soldier; gave it a cordial grip; made an abortive attempt to say something neat and appropriate; and broke abruptly off at the first word. Then Harrod came back.

"Brandon," said he, "there's the mischief to pay in New Orleans. I've just received the papers, and it looks as though there would be riot and bloodshed with a vengeance."

"What's up now?" I asked, with vivid interest.

"It seems to be a breaking out of the old row. Two legislatures, you know, and a double-headed executive. More troops are ordered there."

I eagerly took the paper and read the headlines. The same old story, only worse and more of it. The State-house beleaguered; the metropolitan police armed with Winchesters and manning a battery; the citizens holding indignation meetings and organizing for defence against usurping State government; two riots on Canal Street, and a member of one legislature shot down by the sergeant-at-arms of the other; a great mob organizing to attack the governor and the State-house, etc., etc. It all looked familiar enough. I had seen the same thing but a short time before. It was simply a new eruption of the old volcano, but a grave one, unless I utterly misjudged the indications.

the old volcano, but a grave one, unless I utterly misjudged the indications.

"Amory," said Harrod, "mount your horse and come over to dinner with us. Mr. Brandon and I must go back, for there are matters in the mail which require my attention at once."

But Amory said he could not leave. In Vinton's absence he felt that he ought to stick to camp. We drove back as we came.

Both the young ladies were on the gallery when we drove up. Harrod shook his head in response to the look of inquiry in Pauline's eyes.

"Not back yet, and no news of him,—unless —unless—there should be something in this letter," said he, with provoking gravity and deliberation, as he felt in every pocket of his garments in apparently vain search, while the quizzical look in his face proclaimed that he was purposely reserving the right pocket for the last.

Miss Summers stood with exemplary patience and outstretched hand. At last the eagerly-expected letter was produced, and Harrod and I went in to talk over the startling tidings from New Orleans. The next moment we heard Pauline's rapid step in the hall and ascending the stairs; heard her go hurriedly to her room and close the door. Harrod looked puzzled and a little worried.

"I hope there is no bad news from Vinton," he said. "That rush to her room is unlike her."

Then the swish of Kitty's skirts was heard. Harrod stepped out and spoke some words to her in a low tone. Her reply was anxious and startled in its hurried intonation, but the words were indistinct.

"She says Pauline did not read her letter through at all, but sprang up with tears in her eyes and merely said she must run up-stairs a few minutes. What do you suppose is wrong?"

Of course I had no explanation to offer. Pauline did not return for an hour. When she again appeared she was very pale and quiet. Harrod meantime had taken a horse and ridden off to Sandbrook, where he wanted to reach the telegraph-office. It was late in the evening when he returned. I had been reading in the library for some time while the ladies were at the piano. He strode into the hall and stood at the parlor-door.

"Pauline, did the major tell you in his letter?" he asked.

"Tell me what?" she inquired, with quickly rising color.

"That their orders had come?" She hesitated and made no reply. Quickly he stepped forward and threw his arm around her, tenderly kissing her forehead.

"You'll make a soldier's wife, Pauline. You can keep a secret."

And now, looking quickly at Miss Kitty, I saw

that she had risen and was eagerly gazing at them, a strange, wistful light in her sweet young face.

"What is it all, colonel?" I inquired.

"The cavalry left for New Orleans at dark. Amory got telegraphic orders soon after we left, and Vinton came in from the West by the evening train and took command at the station. Neither of them had time to come out here to say good-by," he added, with an involuntary glance at Kitty, while still holding Pauline's hand in his own.

"You saw Major Vinton?" Pauline calmly asked.

"Yes, dear. I have a note for you. He was only there thirty minutes. Amory had the troop, horses and all, on the cars before the Memphis train got in."

She took her note and with him walked into the library. Irresolutely I stepped out on the gallery a moment. Then returning for a cigar or something consolatory, I nearly collided with Miss Kitty at the parlor-door. She recoiled a pace; then with her bonny head bowed in her hands, with great sobs shaking her slender form, my unheroic little heroine rushed past me and up the stairs to her own room. I felt like a spy.

CHAPTER VII.

THE next few days passed somewhat gloomily. Eager interest centred in the daily paper from New Orleans. The *Times* in those days was "run" entirely in the interest of a strong faction not inaptly termed "carpet-baggers." Few of the Republican party of the white element had been natives and property-owners in the State before the war. All of the colored race, most of them at least, had been residents perhaps, but held as property rather than as property-owners. The *Picayune*, always the representative of the old *régime* in the South, was naturally the journal which found its way into our distant household. Its pictures of affairs in the Crescent City were startling beyond question, and its columns were filled with grave portent of riot, insurrection, and bloodshed.

Judge Summers was visibly worried by its reports. Harrod looked gloomy and ill at ease; Pauline very grave; Kitty picturesquely doleful. All, however, seemed to relax no effort to make me feel at home and "entertained," but the evident cloud overshadowed me. I began to want to get away.

If all New Orleans were swept by the flames, my personal losses would be slight; but the small library I owned would be an excuse. My confidence that neither side would set fire to anything was only equalled by that which I felt that both would join forces to put it out if they did. For two years we had been having just the same exhilarating experiences, and it never came to burning anything but a little powder. Sometimes one side, sometimes another would raise a huge mob, and with much pomp and parade, with much blatant speech-making and wide publication of their intentions, would march noisily through the streets towards some public building, at that moment held by the opposite party, avowedly for the purpose of taking it by force of arms. The first year there had been some desultory shooting, but no casualties to speak of. The second there had been less damage, though far more display; for by this time there were three parties in the field. Then, however, Uncle Sam assumed the *rôle* of peace-maker; sent a general thither with his staff (giving him a major-general's title and a major's force), with vague orders as to what he was to do, as I chanced to know, beyond keeping the peace and upholding the law and the constituted authorities. As three parties claimed to be the "constituted authorities," it seemed embarrassing at times to tell which to uphold. Washington officials declined to decide for him, so the veteran soldier hit on the happy expedient of upholding the party that was attacked. This put him squarely in the right so far as keeping the peace was concerned; for whichever crowd sallied forth to whip the other, invariably found a small battalion of bayonets, or on one occasion a solitary aide-de-camp representing the United States. They would not "fire on the flag"; so retired to thunder at one another through the press. But it put him squarely in the wrong where settling the question for good and all was concerned. So long as the factions felt sure they would not be allowed to fight, the more they talked about doing it; and the real sufferers were the patient, plodding infantry officers and men, who were kept trudging up and down, night and day, from town to barracks. They were tired, hungry, jaded-looking fellows that winter. I had called three of them into my room one chill morning after they had been standing all night on the curb-stones of the State-house waiting for an attack they knew would never come; warmed them up with coffee or cocktails as they might prefer; then one of them opened his heart.

"This whole thing is the most infernal farce," said he. "Ten to one the true way to stop it is to send us miles away and let them get at one another. The Lord knows I'd afford them every encouragement. They don't want to fight. If old General Fitz Blazes would only send me with my company *behind* instead of between these howling idiots they'd evaporate quick enough."

Well I recalled every bit of this! It was when the "radical" party was split up into local factions, each demanding the State-house—and the Treasury; but—things were different now. The old residents, the business men, the representative citizens of the city had stood that sort of thing just as long as human endurance and their ebbing purses could stand it. They now had organized and risen against the perturbed State authorities; and when that class of men began shooting somebody was going to be hurt. As yet nothing aggressive had been done; but the Republican government was tottering on its Louisiana throne, and appealed for aid. This it was that was sending troops from all directions to the Crescent City. I decided to go and protect my lares and penates, trivial though they might be.

To my relief, yet surprise, the moment I mentioned this to Colonel Summers his face lighted up with an expression of delight.

"Mr. Brandon, we'll go together, and as soon as you like."

Noticing my evident surprise, he added, "To tell the truth I ought to go, and at once. Will you come into father's library and let me explain?"

Assenting, as a matter of course, I followed him. Pauline was seated by her father's side as we entered, writing, as she often did, from his dictation.

"Father," broke in the colonel, abruptly, "we can spare you all that work. Mr. Brandon tells me he has decided to go at once to New Orleans. I will go with him, and take the papers."

The judge rose somewhat slowly—anxiety had told on him very much in the last day or two—and greeted me with his old-fashioned courtesy.

"It is a source of great regret to me—to us all—that you should leave us; yet you have doubtless anxieties, as indeed I have,—great ones,—and I wish it were in my power to go myself; but that cannot be, for a fortnight at least; and by that time, as things are looking now, it may be too late,—it may be too late. My son will tell you——" he broke off suddenly.

Miss Summers had risen; her sweet, thoroughbred face had grown a little paler of late, and she stood anxiously regarding her father, but saying not a word. For some moments we sat in general conversation; then, noticing how tired the judge was looking, I rose, saying it was time to make preparations.

Two hours later, the old carriage rattled up to the steps. The colonel stood aside, holding some final consultation with his father. Miss Summers, with a blush that was vastly becoming to her, handed me a letter for the major. "As yet, you know, Major Vinton has not been able to send me his New Orleans address. They are barely there by this time; but you were so incautious as to offer to take anything to him, so I burden you with this."

Kitty Carrington was looking on with wistful eyes.

"And you, little lady? what note or message will you intrust to me?"

She had smoothed back her bright hair. She was looking again as she had the night she begged to play nurse over our unconscious Mars. She looked older, graver, but so gentle, so patient in the trouble that had come into her young life. Whatever that trouble might have been *I* could not say. There was something very pathetic about the slender little figure as she stood there.

For all answer to my question, she shook her head, smiling rather sadly, yet striving to throw archness into her accompanying gesture. The faint shrug of her pretty shoulders, the forward movement of her hands, with open and extended palms,—something so Southern in it all. I could not help noting it. Possibly I stared, as previous confessions indicate that I had that adventurous night in the cars.

My rudeness caused her to turn sharply away with heightened color.

Then came general good-byes, good speeds, good lucks, promises to write,—those promises, like so many others, made only to be broken. We clambered into the carriage. Already the driver was gathering his whip and reins; had "chucked" to his sleepy team. Harrod was sitting on the side nearest the group on the steps; I craning my neck forward for a last look at them. Kitty was eagerly bending forward; her lips parted, her eyes dilated, her fingers working nervously. Already the wheels had begun to crunch through the gravel, when with sudden movement she darted like a bird down the steps.

"*Harrod!*" she cried.

"Hold on, driver," was the response, as he bent to the doorway to meet her.

Standing on tiptoe, her tiny white hands clutching his arm, a vivid color shooting over her face, her eyes one moment nervously, apprehensively, reproachfully glancing at me, plainly saying, "Please don't listen," then, raised to his bronzed, tender face, as he bent ear towards her lips in response to the evident appeal. She rapidly whispered half a dozen words. "*Do* you understand? *Sure* you understand?" she questioned eagerly, as now she leaned back, looking up into his eyes.

He bent still farther, kissed her forehead. "Sure," he nodded. "Sure."

Then back she sprang. Crack went the whip, and we rolled away towards the gate.

Looking back, my eyes took in for the last time the old home; and the picture lingers with me, will live with me to the end of my lonely life. The red-gold light of the setting sun streamed in all its glory on the southern front of the quaint plantation house. The tangled shrubbery, the sombre line of the dense forest beyond the fields, the vines and tendrils that clung about the gallery railing and the wooden pillars, the low-hanging eaves, the moss-covered line of porch-roof,—all were tinged, gilded, gleaming here and there with the warmth and glow of the gladness-giving rays. The windows above blazed with their reflected glory. Even old Blondo's curly hide and Jake Biggs's woolly pate gained a lustre they never knew before. All around the evidences of approaching decay and present dilapidation, so general throughout the bright sunny South years after the war, all around the homeliest objects, the wheelbarrow and garden tools, there clung a tinge of gladness in answering homage to the declining king of day; but, central figures of all, the trio we left upon the steps, *they* fairly stood in a halo of mellow gold. The gray-haired gentleman waving his thin hand in parting salutation; the noble, womanly girl at his side, half supporting, half leaning upon him; and on the lower stair, kissing her hand, waving her dainty kerchief, her eyes dancing, her cheeks aflame, her white teeth flashing through the parted lips, her fragile form all radiance, all sweet, glowing, girlish beauty, stood Kitty Carrington; she who but a moment before had seemed so patiently sad.

"Did you ever see anything prettier?" I gasped, as at last the winding roadway hid them from our sight.

"Kitty, Brandon?—she's a darling!" was the warm-hearted answer.

That was precisely my opinion.

All the way into Sandbrook I was tortured with curiosity to know the purport of the mysterious parting whisper. It would not do to let Colonel Summers suspect that of me; neither would it answer to propound any question. We had much to talk of that is of no interest and has no bearing on our story, but it kept us employed until we reached the station.

Our train was due at 7.45, going west, the same hour at which the troops had left. Their single passenger-car and the four freight-cars on which their horses were carried had been coupled to the regular train. They had gone, we learned, to Grand Junction; thence down the Mississippi Central. The station-master was an old army friend of the colonel's. He received us with all courtesy, and immediately asked us into his own little office.

"Reckon you'd best just make yourselves comfortable, gentlemen; that train's nigh onto two hours late, near as I can make it."

"Two hours late! Why, that will ruin our connection!" exclaimed Harrod.

"They're going to try and make the Central wait over," was the answer, "but I'd bet high on our being later'n we think for. Once a fellow gets off his schedule on this road, he's more apt to be losing all the time than gaining."

The colonel and I looked at each other a moment in some dismay. Quandary though it was, there was nothing for it but to wait, and wait we did, two—three hours. The darkness grew intense back towards the Tennessee; the loungers in the waiting-room or platform in groups of two or three, rose, yawned, stretched themselves, "'Lowed t'warn't no use waitin'; could see the derned train any other night just as well," and took themselves and their tobacco-juice off. The lights across the way, beyond the tracks, died out one by one, until only those two were left which represented the rival saloons, still keeping open for the presumable benefit of some prowler hoping to get trusted for a drink. Finally only the station-master and ourselves were left, all drowsy, but the former still seated, with his one remaining hand close to his telegraph instrument. Still no news of the train. I began to doze.

It could not have been more than ten or fifteen minutes before the clicking of the instrument aroused me. Having long since ceased to care whether the train now came or not, since we had heard by nine that the Central would not wait, I only sleepily gazed at the operator. The colonel had gone asleep, and the sound did not awake him. But another moment the expression on the face of the man sitting so intently over his table aroused me to eagerness. At first professionally indifferent, it grew suddenly clouded; then a look of keen distress came upon it as he quickly glanced around at his old comrade.

I involuntarily sprang up and approached the table. He had written half the message, then dropped pencil and hammered away at the key.

"For him," said he, with a backward jerk of the head to indicate the colonel.

It seemed an endless time before he could get the thing straightened out and the message written.

"Please wake him," said he.

I gently shook Harrod's shoulder. He started up with soldierly promptitude.

"Train coming?" he asked, as be began gathering his traps.

"Not yet, colonel. It's news from the boys, the cavalry."

"Got to New Orleans all right?"

"Got there; but—read for yourself."

With a face that paled even in the dim light of the station, and lips that trembled under his moustache, the colonel read, handed it to me without a word, and turned away.

This was the message:

"NEW ORLEANS, Tuesday.
"COLONEL H. SUMMERS, Sandbrook Station, M. and C. R. R., Alabama.
"Arrived yesterday. Vinton dangerously ill; delirious. Post surgeons in charge. If possible, come.
"FRANK AMORY."

Then we three looked at one another with faces sad and blanched. Harrod was the first to speak.

"May I take your horse, Billy?"

"Yes, and the house and barn if it'll help."

"Then I'm off for home at once, for Pauline."

The delay of that train was a blessing in disguise.

CHAPTER VIII.

A DIM, murky morning it was that dawned on Sandbrook the following day. I had spent the livelong night at the station. The missing train came unheeded, soon after Colonel Summers on "Billy's" horse loped off into the northern darkness. I had sent a dispatch to Amory, care of Department Headquarters in New Orleans. "Billy" had hospitably invited me to share his humble breakfast, made most relishable though by the steaming coffee "cooked" army fashion in a battered old pot with a reliable lid. I had noted with respect and with pleasure the fine picture of General Lee hanging over the narrow mantel, and the battered old cavalry sabre beneath it; and was beginning to ask myself how I could best employ the day until evening train-time, when the rapid beat of hoofs and the familiar rattle of the carriage-wheels sounded in my ears.

"Hyar they come," said "Billy." "I knew they would."

Even before we could reach the platform, the carriage had whirled up there and Harrod sprang from the box-seat.

"That freight gone by yet, Billy?"

"The freight! Lord, no! Colonel, you're not going to take Miss Summers that way?"

"It hasn't gone, dear," he quickly spoke to the silent inmate of the carriage. "But it's due how soon?" turning again to his friend.

"Ten minutes, colonel, and on time, too, if you're bound to go by her."

"By all means. We may strike something at Corinth; if not, we'll go on to the Junction." Then with lowered voice, "Anything is better than waiting at such a time. We'd better get them out, I think."

Them! Who could be there? thought I, for up to this time I had thought best not to intrude. Now I stepped forward as he opened the carriage-door, and with light, quick spring out popped Kitty.

"Mr. Brandon will take charge of you, Kit; there's a dear," said he, gently, then turned again to the door, and tenderly handed out his sister. She came instantly to me with dry eyes, and firm, low voice, only with face so pale. She frankly held forth her hand, which—which I took in both my own.

"Have you heard anything further?"

I shook my head.

"And you have been sitting up here all night waiting for us How kind, yet how tired you must be!"

"I never expected you till evening," I answered, bluntly, and was rewarded by a look of quick, reproachful surprise.

"Harrod reached us at one o'clock. It took very little time to get ready. Mr. Brandon, can you make *any* conjecture as to the nature of his illness?"

"None whatever; fever of some kind, I am half inclined to believe, contracted while off on this court-martial tour."

She bowed her head, and now silent tears fell from her eyes. Harrod led her to one side and, putting his arm around her, stood whispering cheeringly to her. Then I turned to Kitty, who was very quietly engaged in getting out satchels, baskets, and travelling-bags; all was done before I reached her.

"It is a surprise to see you, Miss Kitty."

"A surprise! Surely you did not suppose I would let Paulie go on so sad a journey without me. There are many ways in which I can help her."

There was no answer to the wisdom of that statement. The distant whistle of the freight had twice been heard, and in ten minutes our party of four were disposed in the conductor's caboose. The situation had been explained to that officer in very few words by Harrod and "Billy;" and, with that almost chivalrous courtesy which the roughest-looking men in the South show to the gentler sex on all occasions I ever witnessed, the train-hands had busied themselves in making a comfortable corner for the ladies. Rude and poor were the appliances, but Walter Raleigh never laid down his priceless cloak for foot of royal mistress with truer grace than did those rough ex-soldiers spread their blankets, coats, and pillows to make a soft substructure for the heavy shawls which the ladies had with them. Watching, as I have on a thousand occasions, the gentle courtesy of Southern men to women, high or low, I never lack for explanation, never wonder how they came to fight so well. Bayard Taylor struck the key-note when he wrote,—

"The bravest are the tenderest,
The loving are the daring."

At noon we were at Corinth and eagerly questioning the officials there. No train till nine.

"What chance by going to Grand Junction?"

"No better, colonel; they've had the customary smash-up on the Central, and 'taint no use trying. Even if the road weren't blocked, their south-bound express don't get off as early as ours from here."

"Are there no trains coming south, not even freight?"

"Colonel, I'm sorry, but there's not a train of any kind,—nothin' except a special, going through a-whoopin' for Orleans, I suppose, with a lot o' damyankees."

"What! a special with troops, do you mean?" asked Harrod, eagerly.

"Exactly; somewhere from up in Tennessee. Two or three companies—but, Lord! you couldn't ride with them even if they'd let you. They telegraphed ahead here for coffee for seventy men, and want to take the kettles on to the next station. Not much——"

"Never mind, Mr. Agent," broke in Harrod, impatiently; "when are they due?"

"Coffee's ordered for 12.30. Reckon they'll be along very soon," replied the nettled functionary.

"What say you, Brandon? Shall we try it?"

"Most assuredly; and I think it can be done."

Four pairs of anxious, eager eyes watched that train of "damyankees" as it came rushing into the station sharp at 12.30. A crowd of sullen-looking "white trash" had gathered, a larger knot of curious and eager darkies, to see the sight. The engine whizzed past the platform; then two passenger-cars, from every window of which protruded blue-capped, dust-begrimed soldier heads; sentries stood at the doors, and only as the last car—a third passenger-car—came opposite us did the train stop. A sharp, business-like young fellow, in dust-covered fatigue dress with infantry shoulder-straps and cap, sprang out.

"That coffee ready?" he asked, bounding at the agent at once.

"Wall, I s'pose so," drawled the party addressed, as though desirous of giving all the annoyance he could.

"If you want your money you'd better know, and lively too. We've no time to waste. Tumble out here, Sergeant Triggs. Bring six men while this party is waking up."

Then as his men went into the kitchen to bring out the steaming caldrons, I asked if I could see the commanding officer on immediate and important business.

"Certainly, sir; rear car. Come this way."

We followed him, Harrod and I; found the forward half of the third car filled, as were the other two, with the rank and file. At the rear end were half a dozen sleepy, dusty, and disgusted-looking gentlemen.

"This is Major Williams, sir," said the business-like youngster, and in an instant he was out on the platform again.

A tall, dust-colored officer rose to meet my extended card and hand, mild surprise in his eyes. "Major," said I, "Major Vinton, of the cavalry, lies dangerously ill in New Orleans. He is engaged to the sister of my friend, Colonel Summers. No train leaves here until nine to-night, and in our eagerness to get to Vinton before it be too late we ask to be taken with you."

For an instant the commanding officer was staggered by my impetuous harangue, but "he rallied."

"Major Vinton, say you? I'm distressed to hear it. I know him well by reputation, though it has not been my good fortune to meet him. We—we must find some way—— Excuse me, let me speak one instant with the quartermaster."

He quickly stepped to a bulky, stolid-looking youth, and addressed him in few rapid words. The whistle blew,—my heart stood still. He sprang to a window, stuck out his head, and shouted,—

"A—a—Mr. *Turpin*. Stop the train. Don't start till I tell you."

"All right, sir," came back in the quick, sharp tones we had heard before.

Again the major and the stolid youth met. We heard snatches of the latter's words,—" no precedent, no authority,"—and my heart again sank. Like Mr. Perker of blessed memory, I was about to interpose with "But my dear sir, my *dear* sir," when Mr. Turpin burst in like a thunder-clap at the rear door.

"Jupiter Ammon, fellows! Blow the dust from your eyes if you want to see the prettiest girl in the South!"

"Never mind precedent; we'll make a precedent," broke in the major, impatiently. "Gentlemen,"—he turned to us,—"you see how forlorn are our surroundings, but you and yours are welcome." The whole thing took less time than it takes to read it.

Harrod sprang for his sister. Mr. Turpin sprang for Kitty. Eager hands seized the bags and traps, shoving them through windows, anywhere, anyhow; and half bewildered, all grateful, all surprise, Pauline and Kitty found themselves aboard, and we were spinning out of inhospitable Corinth.

"Pardon our great haste, ladies," I heard the major saying. "We *must* be in New Orleans some time in the early morning." The "damyankees" were going to get us there twenty-four hours ahead of any other arrangement we could have made.

Shall I ever forget that almost breathless ride? "Be here to-morrow morning without fail" were the words of the dispatch Major Williams had received at the point where his train left the Louisville road and swung into the rails of the Mobile and Ohio. It was the "longer way round,"—that through Mobile,—but some late experiences had proved it the shorter way home; and, as the conductor presently explained to the major, on entering the car, "I've given the engineer orders to jump her for all she's worth. We only stop for water and passing one up-train. Even the express has to side-track for us."

Then the conductor wiped his hot brow, and with infinite surprise looked first at the ladies just getting settled into the seats eager hands had been dusting and preparing for them, then at me. Then Harrod came quickly to us, and in him he recognized at once Colonel Summers of the Alabama cavalry of by-gone days. With the Freemasonry of old campaigners, they gripped hands before questions of any kind were put. Harrod promptly explained the situation. "Thanks to these gentlemen, we are permitted to share their car. Of course we settle with you for the fare. But for their kindness we could not have reached New Orleans before late, perhaps too late, to-morrow night."

The conductor turned to the officers: "Major Williams, sir (yes, he did say "sah," and I liked to hear it), I want to thank you in the name of the road for your prompt courtesy to these friends of mine. I had to jump for the telegraph-office myself, and did not see them. You can just bet your life, sir, the Mobile and Ohio shall know of it, and they'll thank you in a way I'm not empowered to."

And so, whizzing at forty-five miles an hour. Southron and Yank were drawing into the brotherhood of a common sympathy.

And so it went all through that grimy afternoon. With what unremitting thoughtfulness and care those fellows looked after our fair charges! The sanctity of her grief and anxiety rendered Miss Summers the object of the deepest respect and sympathy. Reclining at the rear of the car, her veil drawn over her face, none but Harrod ventured to approach her; but Kitty was the centre of incessant attention, and through her all manner of improvised delicacies were brought to Pauline. The dust was stifling, and indefatigable Mr. Turpin appeared from somewhere in front with a tin basin filled with cracked ice. The doctor came forward with a silver cup of delicious lemonade (he had levied on his pannier for lime-juice and powdered sugar) dexterously rendered soulful by a dash of Vini Gallici. Kitty smiled her thanks to both, and a duplicate of the beverage was grateful to her silent cousin. We flew over the rattling rails, and the jarring was incessant. The doctor produced an air-pillow for Pauline's head. We stopped somewhere for water, and the major disappeared. The ladies had brought luncheon in a large basket—but no appetites. The soldiers had rations and were filled. The officers had not had a mouthful since a breakfast at 3 A.M., and were hungry. No chance for a bite until 5 P.M., when, said the conductor, they might grab a sandwich at Ragsdale's, at Meridian. "But we can't stop three minutes, boys." Kitty overheard it. She was in animated conversation with a tall subaltern, who claimed to be from Kentucky. They were sitting three seats ahead of Miss Summers, who was undisturbed by their chatter; all voices were subdued as far as was possible. Mr. Turpin, who was a man of few words but vast action, was hovering about, eager for a chance to do something. She knew it. They all seem to have infinite intuition that way.

"Oh, Mr. Turpin, would you please bring me our lunch-basket?" And Turpin was down upon us like his namesake of old, demanding the basket in a manner suggestive of "or your lives." Another second and it was deposited in front of her, and she bade him summon his brotherhood; and they went, even the stolid quartermaster, who felt sheepish apparently. And there she sat like a little Lady Bountiful, dispensing to each and all (a Southern lunch-basket reminds me of the parable of the loaves and fishes), and they surrounded her, eating and adoring.

At five we rolled into Meridian, and Ragsdale's sandwiches were forgotten. Major Williams sprang from the train.

"Yes, dear," I heard Harrod saying to his sister, "I will try and send a dispatch from here," and with that he rose. I went with him in search of the telegraph-office. At the door we met the major, some open dispatches in his hand.

"Have we time to send a despatch to New Orleans?" asked Harrod, eagerly.

"Hardly," said the major, with a quiet smile. "But won't this do?" and he placed in Harrod's hand one of the papers. The message read:

"Telegram received. Assure Vinton's friends that fever is less. He receives best care. We are hopeful now.
"REYNOLDS, A.A.G."

"Thank God!" I uttered.

Summers, with tears starting to his eyes, grasped the soldier's hand.

"You are a very thoughtful man, sir."

"All aboard!" yelled the conductor. "Get those lamps lit now."

Somehow I was glad it was dusk in the car as we sprang aboard. Harrod, with quick, eager step, went directly to her. Something told her he had news, and she rose, throwing back her veil, and bent eagerly forward. He placed the paper in her hand, and, clutching it, she seemed to devour the contents. Kitty had turned quickly to look. Conversation somehow had ceased. Then we saw her glance one instant up in his face. Then his strong arms were round her, for, burying her face in his breast, she had burst into a passion of almost hysterical weeping. Then we all turned away and shook hands. The whole car knew Vinton was better. One soldier up in front wanted to give three cheers, but was promptly suppressed. Kitty's own eyes were overflowing as she received the congratulations of the lately banquetted, and with a great load off our hearts we sped onward through the darkness.

Two sweet pictures remain in my memory of that strange night. First was that of Miss Summers and Major Williams. At her request Harrod brought him to her, that she might thank him for the thoughtfulness, the delicate attention he had shown. Her face was exquisite in the revival of hope, in the intensity of gratitude.

The second was about 11 P.M. We had had to make some stops. Our run was now less impeded. It had grown chilly and raw. Coming in from the front, whither I had gone to smoke with the conductor, I found the inmates of the rear of our car apparently buried in slumber, except one figure. Mr. Turpin, with his blouse collar turned up and his hands in his pockets, was sitting bolt upright. Two seats behind him, her fair hair curling about her rounded cheek, sleeping like a babe after all the fatigues and excitements of the day, but from neck to foot completely enveloped in a cloak of army blue, was Kitty Carrington, our rampant little rebel Kit.

CHAPTER IX.

EARLY in the morning, earlier even than I had supposed possible, the conductor's voice was heard announcing to somebody that we would be in New Orleans in less than half an hour. I had been sleeping somewhat uneasily, curled up on one of the seats. I was dimly conscious of the fact that at some unknown hour in the night another telegram had been received referring to Vinton, and that Miss Summers was wide awake when it came. I remember Harrod's bending over and kissing her, and hearing the words, "That is better yet." Then sleep again overpowered me. Now, at daybreak, I arose and gazed around the dimly-lighted car. Miss Summers, Harrod, and Major Williams were the only occupants apparently astir. The former was sitting near the opened window; the cool, salty breeze from the Gulf was playing with the ripples of fair hair that clustered about her forehead. She looked very white and wan in the uncertain light, but there was a womanly tenderness and sweetness about her face that made it inexpressibly lovely to me. She was gazing wistfully out over the sea of marsh and swamp, as though longing to bridge the distance that still separated us from the city, where he lay battling with that insidious enemy. Harrod and the major were in earnest conversation. Other occupants of the car were beginning to stir uneasily, as though warned that soon they must be up and doing; but Kitty still slept, and the cloak of army blue still covered her. Mr. Turpin had disappeared.

A few moments more and the officers had been aroused; the men were donning their belts and equipments; Pauline herself stepped forward, and, bending over her pretty cousin, roused her from her baby-like sleep; and glancing from the windows, I could see that we were rolling up the "Elysian Fields." Then came the curving sweep around on the broad levee. All looked quiet, even deserted, as we passed the Mint and the wide thoroughfare of Esplanade Street. Some of the lamps still burned dimly in the *cafés* and bars, but no trace of commotion or excitement could be discerned. It was with some little surprise then that our eyes met the warlike scene as we rolled into the station at the foot of Canal Street.

The instant the train stopped, our car was boarded by an alert gentleman in civilian dress whom I had often seen, and whom I knew to be an aide-de-camp on the staff of the commanding general. He came at once to Major Williams;

shook hands with him, and conveyed some orders in a low tone of voice; then asked to be presented to Colonel Summers. Major Williams brought him to where our group of four was then standing, at the rear of the car,—Miss Summers, Kitty, Harrod, and myself.

"Let me introduce Colonel Newhall, of General Emory's staff," he said, and the colonel, raising his hat in general salutation to the party, spoke in the hurried, nervous way I afterwards found was habitual with him, despite the *sang-froid* that distinguished him at all times save in the presence of ladies.

"I have come direct from Major Vinton's room, Colonel Summers, and am happy to tell you that the doctors pronounce him much better. The general charged me to bring you the latest news of him, and to express to you and to your ladies his warm interest and sympathy."

Then we had not come as strangers to a strange land. I glanced at Pauline, as her brother, warmly grasping the staff-officer's hand, presented him to her and to Kitty. Her clear, brave eyes were suffused with tears and she did not venture to speak a word; but she was infinitely moved by the constantly recurring evidences of interest in her and her gallant lover. Such an informal announcement of an engagement perhaps was not strictly in accordance with the prevailing customs of society, but the exigencies of the case put all such considerations aside. Everybody on our train knew the story of course, and it had evidently been telegraphed to headquarters. Meantime, Major Williams had been superintending the debarkation of his men, and they were forming ranks on the platform outside. Beyond them, a long line of stacked arms was guarded by sentries, and several companies of infantry were grouped behind them, watching with professional interest the arrival of comrade soldiery. A number of officers had gathered at the side of the car,—very weary they looked too, and far from jaunty in their dusty fatigue uniforms; but they were intent on welcoming Major Williams and his command, and at that hour in the morning, costume and unshaven chins were not subject to criticism. Time and again it had been my lot to be at this very station, but never before had I seen it thronged with troops. It was evident that matters of grave moment were going on in the city.

Colonel Newhall had left the car for a moment and Harrod came to me:

"It seems that Vinton is at Colonel Newhall's quarters on Royal Street, Mr. Brandon. He met the troop on its arrival in town, and finding Vinton wellnigh delirious with fever, had him taken at once to his lodgings. There are a number of vacant rooms, he tells me, and he has made all arrangements to take us right there; so there we will go. The St. Charles is crowded, and Pauline naturally wants to be near him. I think it the best arrangement that could possibly be made."

Even as he finished, the colonel came in to say that the carriage was ready. Harrod, Pauline, Kitty and I followed him to the platform. The group of officers standing there courteously raised their forage-caps as our ladies passed them. Kitty looked furtively about her as she stepped from the car, and Mr. Turpin sprang forward to take her light satchel. It was but a few steps to the carriage. Pauline and Kitty were handed in. Summers and Colonel Newhall took their seats in the carriage. We shook hands all round without saying much of anything, except that I should meet them later in the day; the driver cracked his whip, and away they went up Canal Street, Mr. Turpin and I gazing after them.

Even as we looked, there came trotting down the stone pavement towards us a pair of cavalrymen. The one in front, tall, slender, erect, I recognized at once as Frank Amory. The one in rear was evidently his orderly. Never noticing the carriage, which had hurried off on the Custom-House side of the street, the former rode rapidly to the very point where we were standing. I saw Mr. Turpin look eagerly at him, then spring forward.

"Sheep, old man, how are you?"

"Hello, Cyclone! when did you get here?"

and throwing the reins to his orderly, Frank Amory sprang from the saddle, and warmly grasped Mr. Turpin by the hand. The boys were classmates.

It was perhaps a minute before Amory noticed that I was standing there, so absorbed was he in greeting his comrade. The moment he caught sight of me, however, he stepped quickly forward. Quite a number of the younger officers had gathered around by this time, and with heightened color he looked eagerly in my face.

"When did you come? Who—who else came?" he asked, excitedly.

"We arrived only a few minutes ago," I said. "Miss Summers, Miss Kitty, and the colonel with me. They just drove off in that carriage. We are so rejoiced to hear Major Vinton is better."

"You don't say so!" he exclaimed, then stopped short, as though at a loss what to add. "I—I had no idea she—you could get here so soon. Vinton *is* better, thank God! Where have they gone?"

"To Colonel Newhall's quarters," I answered. "It seems there are several rooms, and the colonel says his landlady will take the best of care of them. Then they will be near him, which is something to be considered."

"Why, Sheep, did you know Colonel Summers and Miss Carrington?" broke in Mr. Turpin, suddenly.

"Yes, quite well. I was stationed near them," was the answer, given with some constraint.

Mr. Turpin stuck his hands deep in his pockets and said not another word. Other officers crowded about Mr. Amory to inquire for Major Vinton, and to ask for news. Presently Major Williams came up with Colonel Starr, the commanding officer of the battalion that was "in bivouac" at the station, and I was presented to the latter. From them I learned something of the situation.

They had been on guard all night there at the station. What for they could not exactly tell. It seems that one faction of the Legislature occupied the temporary State-House; another had its headquarters over a prominent bar-room in Royal Street; and a large concourse of citizens had organized with military formalities and the avowed intention of dislodging the factional Legislature from the house; installing a Governor of their own choice; and subduing the police force of the city, now enrolled as a uniformed and fully-equipped battalion of infantry, with a battery of field-guns and a squadron of cavalry as assistants. The police held the various stations, and no encounter had taken place; but the citizens had turned out in great numbers, and the chances were that they would prove too powerful for the mixed array of the police force; and trouble had been anticipated for that very night, but it had not come. A strong battalion of infantry was posted here at the railway station. Another, after a day of weary marching, was resting at a large cotton-press up the levee; two companies of cavalry were stationed at the quartermaster's warehouse up in Magazine Street, near the headquarters of the commanding general, and two foot batteries from an artillery regiment had spent the night in the State-House itself. Cavalry patrols had been scouting through the city all night, promptly reporting any unusual gathering, but in no case interfering. Verily these were strange accompaniments to the times of piping peace.

It was after seven o'clock when I reached my rooms. I was tired and ought to have been sleepy after the long, rapid ride by rail, but the morning papers were full of exciting prophecy as to the events of the day, and sleep was out of the question. Amory had declined my invitation to breakfast, saying that he could not be away from his troop more than fifteen minutes at a time, and had only managed to get down to the station while out looking after his patrols. A bath and a change of raiment proved refreshing. Then I took a car; rode to Canal Street; walked down Royal to Colonel Newhall's lodgings; met one of the doctors, who assured me that Major Vinton was doing very well, and that later they hoped he might be well enough to see

Miss Summers. He was still flighty and had no idea of his whereabouts. The ladies were upstairs resting. Would I see them? No, I preferred not to disturb them, and so went off by myself to breakfast at my usual haunt, Moreau's. The room was already well filled when I entered. Most of the tables were occupied, many of them by prominent citizens. Much earnest talk was going on in subdued tones, and there was an air of suppressed excitement that was noticeable to the most careless observer. Two of the tables were occupied by a party of infantry officers whom I had seen at the station, and it was noticeable that within earshot of them little was being said in reference to "the situation." I had several acquaintances among the business men present, and took a seat near them. The first words that fell upon my ears were,—

"And it will be done to-night, you may depend upon it."

"But do you suppose that General Emory will stand by and allow such a thing to go on under his very nose?"

"General Emory can't help himself, sir. His orders from Washington do not permit him to act unless called upon by the marshal or by the State authorities. The whole thing will be over and done with before they can make their demand, and our people will have dispersed before the troops get there."

"But suppose they get wind of it and call upon him to station his men to meet the move?"

"Why, that ends it, of course. We are helpless in that case. We don't mean to raise a finger against the general government. Let him send a corporal's guard to any one of the places and it's safe; but as for this infernal mottled police——"

"Steady!"

And then both speakers looked up at the party of infantry officers, who had risen and were quietly leaving. Then they looked at me, and the rest of the conversation was in too low a tone for any one to hear.

The day was one of restless anxiety, yet of apparent quiet and order. The broad "banquette" of Canal Street was thronged with ladies and children as is customary on bright afternoons. The matinées at the Varieties and the St. Charles Theatre were crowded. At half-past four, as I strolled up the street under the friendly shade of the awnings, that made the wide sidewalks one long arcade, I was struck by the perfectly peaceful aspect of the scene. From the Custom-House to Rampart Street, on the lower side of the way, I did not see a policeman, much less a soldier in uniform; but at all the corners, the knots of unoccupied men were much larger than usual; this being especially the case around Dumonteil's and Lopez's confectioneries, and the well-known establishment of "Dr. Sample."

On the opposite side and grouped around the brown-stone building of the Shakespeare Club, half a dozen men in civilian dress were lolling about, and less than one hundred yards up Dryades Street, as many more were sitting or standing around the entrance of the massive Mechanics' Institute, now used as a State-House and place of meeting of one at least of the rival Legislatures; but there was nothing in its exterior to indicate the state of siege as described in the daily press. In all, there might have been one hundred loungers scattered from Victor's marble-columned restaurant on the lower side down to "Dr. Sample's," in the middle of the next block; but absolute quiet and order reigned. Some of the windows in the second story of the Institute were open, and occasionally the features of some colored legislator could be seen peering curiously and cautiously out towards Canal Street.

Now that demon of curiosity that has always possessed me, prompted me to stroll across the broad thoroughfare and to approach the entrance of Dryades Street. As a neutral, I felt serenely confident that neither side would take exceptions to my movements, but looking behind me as I reached the car-tracks, I saw that the listless loungers on the banquette had crowded forward to its edge, and were watching me with interest. Keeping on, however, I soon reached the upper side, and deliberately walked ahead as though bent on going to the State-House. The instant I got beyond the Canal Street pavement, however, one of the men I had noticed at the upper corner stepped quickly in front of me and said,—

"Pardon me, Mr. Brandon, where did you wish to go?" Then, seeing my look of surprise, he smilingly added, "Of course I know you, sir, though you do not know me; I'm a detective."

"Why," said I, "if there be no objections, I would like to go to the State-House, just to see what is going on."

"I'm sorry, sir," was the civil reply; "at this moment our orders are to admit nobody."

Now, I hated to go back. I knew well that all those estimable fellow-citizens of mine on the other side were watching the scene, and that they would be sure to hold me in lighter estimation if I had to retire. I put a bold face on the matter and whipped out my card-case.

"There are two batteries of foot artillery in there, I'm told, and among their officers is a gentleman whom I used to know in New York and would like to see. Can you send this to him?" I hastily scrawled "Late N. Y. 7th Regt." under my name. The detective took the card; whistled to a boy who stood near; the youngster seized it and was off like a shot;

while my detective and I walked slowly towards the building. Before we reached the stone steps, a fine-looking fellow in the fatigue uniform of the United States artillery came out and looked inquiringly around. I stepped forward at once and introduced myself; was most courteously greeted and invited to walk in; the police official smilingly nodded "All right now," and, guided by the lieutenant, I entered the mysterious portals of the besieged halls of government.

It was an extraordinary sight that met my eyes. Grouped inside the vestibule, where they could not be seen from Canal Street, or indeed from any point on Dryades except directly in front, were some fifty Metropolitan police in complete uniform and the equipments of infantry soldiers; belts, cartridge-boxes, bayonet-scabbards, and all. Their officers, with drawn swords and wearing shoulder-straps like those of the regular service, were gathered in front. Stacks of Winchester rifles stood close by, many of the men having their muskets still in their hands. All the lower hall and the staircases were crowded with these improvised troops, some white, some colored, there being white men in the rank and file, and colored men among the officers. All were very quiet, orderly, and apparently well disciplined. Some of those who were seated on the stairway rose rather slowly to make way for us, and a colored officer in the shoulder-straps of a captain spoke in a quick, sharp tone to them; and, black and white, they sprang to their feet and respectfully drew aside. At the head of the stairs were sentries and an officer of the guard, all in police uniform, and they saluted my artillery guide with all the precision of regulars.

"Would you like to look in at your Legislature?" asked he, with a mischievous grin. I assented. The officer of the guard opened a door, and we found ourselves in an inner hall or vestibule. Here we came upon a dozen colored men surrounding a low wooden counter or table covered with pies, cakes, sandwiches, and fruit. Behind the counter sat an old negress in vehement expostulation.

"It's no use talkin', gen'lemen, you's just wastin' yo' time. Las' year I done trus' de gen'lemen of de Senate an' Representives, an' dey ain't paid me yit."

"But fo' de Lawd's sake, Mis' Fontelieu, I ain't had nuffin to eat sence day befo' yis'day mawnin', an' I's starvin', I is. Yo' ought ter have some consideration fo' gen'lemen of de Legislature what's sufferin' here fo' you an' de people. Soon's we done git our salaries we's goin' to pay you fus' thing. Ain't we, gen'lemen?" said the spokesman appealingly to his brother Solons.

"Of co'se we is, Mis' Fontelieu," was the

chorus, but all to no purpose. Miss Fontelieu's experiences with previous Legislatures and legislators had undermined her faith in the stability of their financial condition, and nothing but cash in hand would induce her to part with any of her stock in trade.

"I'd buy them a breakfast myself," said my lieutenant, laughingly, "for I know very well that they have had nothing to eat except what they could pick up here; but we contributed all our spare greenbacks yesterday, and they'd be just as hungry by ten o'clock to-night."

We pushed on through the lobby and entered the main room, the temporary hall of representatives, and here another odd sight greeted our eyes.

The room was large, rectangular in shape; a raised platform being at the farther end; rows of cane-bottomed chairs were arranged in semicircular order across the hall; a desk for the presiding officer was on the platform; and tables and desks for clerks and reporters stood below it. Scattered in groups all about the room were upwards of an hundred men, some white, some colored, stretched at length upon the chairs, others were lying asleep. The instant we entered, conversation ceased, and all looked eagerly and inquiringly at my companion; even some of the recumbent figures straightened up and gazed at him. Several stepped forward from the nearest group and asked if there were any news, receiving with evident disappointment his civil reply that he had heard nothing.

"They have been cooped up here for nearly forty-eight hours," the lieutenant explained. "You see, they've just got a quorum, and the Governor knows blessed well that if they once get out, the chances are ten to one they'll never get back. Either the other crowd will mob them, or, in fear of the attack on the State-House, they will keep in hiding somewhere around town."

The Governor, with his officers, was in his private room down-stairs, my friend explained; and the Senate was likewise blockaded in another part of the building; and this was the shape in which one Governor, at least, of the sovereign State of Louisiana was "holding the fort" against all would-be adversaries.

Then we left the hall of unwilling representatives; clambered another flight of stairs, and came upon what the local press had not inaptly termed "the citadel." Here, in an upper room, half a dozen officers of artillery of the regular service were killing time, reading, writing, or dozing; and most disgusted they looked with their occupation. On being presented to the commanding officer and his comrades I was courteously greeted and invited to make myself at home, "if," said the major, "you can find any comfort in the situation. I've only once in my life been on more distasteful duty, and that was when we were sent to break up illicit distilleries in Brooklyn."

Their orders, I learned, were that both officers and men should remain in the State-House, and not leave, even for meals, which were to be sent from a neighboring restaurant; and there they had been for two nights and days, in readiness to defend the place if attacked, yet having every assurance that so long as there remained a "regular" soldier in the building it would not be molested. No wonder they yawned and looked bored to death; and my proffer of services was gladly accepted. "Send us anything you may have in the way of reading matter, and we'll be only too thankful," was the major's half-laughing, half-rueful reply, and after an hour's chat I left. The lieutenant accompanied me to the entrance, where he bade me good-by. The knot of detectives drew aside and passed me out without remark. Once more I crossed Canal Street, and in an instant found myself surrounded by a bevy of eager reporters, note-book and pencil in hand, clamoring for information. From the obscurity of yesterday, Mr. G. S. Brandon had suddenly leaped into prominence.

CHAPTER X.

AT nine o'clock that evening I was seated on a balcony overhanging Royal Street, quietly chatting with Miss Summers, Kitty Carrington, and Harrod. Vinton was much better, the doctors had assured us; the fever was broken; he had recognized Pauline during the afternoon, and was now asleep. The doctor had advised her to lie down and rest, for, after all her anxiety and the excitement of her rapid journey, she was looking very white and wan; but after an hour in her room she had again appeared, pleading that she could not sleep, and Harrod had led her out to the balcony, where we sat enjoying the evening air. Colonel Newhall had not returned from headquarters. We saw him for an instant at Moreau's, whither Harrod, Kitty, and I had gone for dinner, about six o'clock, leaving Pauline to share the simple tea offered her by the sympathetic landlady. He had stopped just long enough to say that it was not probable that he would be home during the evening,—he was needed at the office,—and then had walked briskly away. Coming home we could not help noticing how many men there were standing in quiet groups about the Clay statue and all along Canal Street; but Royal Street, generally so busy and bustling, was strangely quiet, wellnigh deserted. It was an exquisite night; the moon was at her full, and objects across the narrow thoroughfare were almost as distinct as in broad daylight. I could easily read the signs over the shops, and distinguish the features of the few people who passed. It was very still, too. Off to our left, towards Canal Street, the roar of wheels over the massive pavement was to be heard, but few sounds broke the stillness near our balcony. Some distance down the street a clear, ringing voice was carolling the page's song from "Mignon"; across the way two or three darkies were chattering in that indescribable language that sounds like French, yet is no more French than Siamese, the *patois* of the Creole negroes; but not a wheel or hoof awakened the echoes of the compact rows of old-fashioned houses.

Our landlady came out and looked uneasily up and down.

"I'm sure I don't know what to make of this," said she. "Ordinarily Royal Street is gay in the evening. To-night it is still as a cemetery. I know something is going to happen. A neighbor of mine on Chartres Street, just back of us, says that hundreds of men have been going down there for the last hour,—going down towards Jackson Square,—and they had guns, most all of them."

It was just then that somewhere near us a clock began striking nine.

Hardly had the last stroke died, quivering away through the still night air, when from the direction of the great cathedral, opposite the very square she named, there came a sudden and startling uproar, a rattling volley of small-arms, a chorus of yells that made the welkin ring; then a pandemonium of shots, shouts, and yells all together. Instantly, people below could be seen rushing to close their shutters; the chattering darkies disappeared around the corner, and we had sprung to our feet and were listening excitedly to the clamor, which increased with every moment. Pauline quickly stepped in-doors; her first thought was for her lover, and she had gone to his door. Kitty, very pale, was grasping the balcony rail and looking appealingly up in Harrod's face. He and I gazed questioningly at each other. Full a minute we stood there before any one spoke. Then Harrod pointed up Royal Street.

"Look! What is this?"

Leaning over the balcony I gazed eagerly up towards the white colonnade of the St. Charles, glistening and brilliant in the moonlight. Coming towards us in perfect silence at rapid, shuffling step, with the moonbeams glancing from their sloping arms and glistening bayonets, was a column of soldiers. Another moment and they were directly under us, and with them, drawn by horses, was a large field-piece. I recognized the uniforms at a glance: they were the police. Rapidly, almost at double-quick, they filed under the balcony and marched on down the street. We followed them with our eyes until they turned to the right, some squares farther east, and waited further developments. The noise of the firing, the shouts and yells had partially died away, but not entirely. Suddenly there came a renewal of the clangor; the rattling fusilade was resumed, then came a volley or two, delivered as though by word of command; then a deafening roar that shook the windows.

"By Jove, Brandon, I can't stand this," said Colonel Summers. "I *must* go and see what it means." Then came another tremendous bang. "That's a twelve-pounder!"

But Kitty and the landlady implored him not to go, and as a final compromise the latter agreed to guide him through her premises to her neighbor's house on Chartres Street, where he could find out all that was going on without being exposed to the danger of the street; and in a few moments more we were both, he and I, standing on a balcony that overhung the latter street. Royal Street had been wellnigh deserted. Chartres Street was a scene of excitement and confusion. Far down to the left we could see the flash of small-arms and hear the shouts of the excited men. Directly under us, numbers of citizens were running, some towards Jackson Square, where the fighting was going on, others towards Canal Street, as though eager to get out of the way. A man living in the house had just come in, pale and panting, and to our quick inquiries he replied that at nine o'clock a great crowd of citizens had suddenly assaulted the police station opposite Jackson Square; had whipped out the police and completely gutted the building; that they had things all their own way until General Badger suddenly appeared with a big gun and a lot of reinforcements, and now there was going to be a tremendous fight. Crowds of citizens were coming from every direction and hemming in the police, and no more reinforcements could reach them, said our informant.

Even as he spoke, we saw a large body of men in civilian garb, but many or most of them armed with shot-guns and rifles, coming up Chartres Street from the Square. Halting at the corner below us, some twenty or thirty of them were told off and left there; the others went on. Their leaders spoke in low tones to the people they met in the street, and the latter turned back as though in implicit obedience. In five minutes, except the silent groups of armed men at the corner, Chartres Street was as deserted as at dawn of day. The firing and noise had ceased.

"There are crowds going down Custom-House Street and the levee," said our still panting friend. "These parties are being thrown out in every direction to prevent more of the police from getting in to help Badger; then in course of an hour we'll have five thousand citizens down there around the Square, and if the United States troops don't interfere it will be all up with the police."

In eager interest Harrod and I waited. Below us the party at the corner had posted two sentinels, who were pacing across the street in most approved soldierly fashion. Every now and then a distant cheer was heard over towards the levee,—fresh bodies of citizens were coming in or somebody was making a speech perhaps. Harrod went back to the house to reassure Pauline, but speedily returned. Vinton was still sleeping quietly, and the doctor was there with the ladies. He said it was understood on the street that at ten o'clock the citizens were going to resume the attack and with every prospect of success. Already they had an overwhelming force.

I looked at my watch. It was just ten minutes of ten. Over on the levee the hoarse shouts of the crowd could be heard at more frequent intervals. Far up the street, towards Canal, I could see a dense black mass blocking the entrance, evidently a crowd of people drawn thither by curiosity, but restrained by a sense of danger from coming farther towards the scene of action. The sentries still paced the streets at the corners above and below us. Two squares farther down towards the cathedral we could see the other sentries pacing to and fro. "Those are the police pickets," said our previous informant; "just wait five minutes and you'll see them skip."

Again I nervously looked at my watch. I was trembling with suppressed excitement. The police station was only four squares away to our left. I thought I could see the moonbeams gleaming on the big gun that our friend and fellow-citizen said the police had run out in the middle of the street and pointed towards the levee.

Suddenly there came a racket towards Canal Street. We all leaned over the balcony and gazed eagerly in that direction. A single black shadow came swiftly down the middle of the street. We heard the loud clatter of iron-shod hoofs on the stone-block pavement. A horseman riding at full gallop came flashing through the moonlight. "Who comes there?" shouted the sentries above us. "Don't stop him!" yelled some authoritative voice as the horseman, never heeding either challenge or rebuke, thundered along almost at racing speed. As he sped under the balcony I did not need to see the glittering aiguillettes and shoulder-knots, or hear the clank of the cavalry sabre, to recognize the youngest of the general's aides-de-camp. Again he was challenged at the lower corner, and some excitable party in the crowd fired a gun. My nerves jumped in quick response, but on went the officer. Then we heard shouts farther down and two more shots, this time from the police, and then Harrod grabbed my arm.

"Come on; let's go and see it. I can't stand this." And leading the way he plunged down the stairs, I following.

"You can't get through there, gentlemen," said the leader of the party below us; "the police hold the street below." So we headed for the levee, two squares away; found a surging crowd there, but, half running, half walking, we pushed ahead, speedily finding ourselves at the outskirts of a great throng of men spreading out over the broad levee towards Jackson Square. Under the gas-lamp at the corner, now surrounded by a dense throng, we could see the aide-de-camp, seated on his panting horse and in animated conversation with some of the citizens nearest him. I had met the young officer and knew him slightly, and was eager to hear what he might say, but it was impossible to get nearer. In a moment, however, he turned away and rode back towards the police station. A tall, gray-headed gentleman, of soldierly bearing and address, stepped upon a box or barrel and spoke briefly to the crowd,—

"Gentlemen,—General Emory sends word that in compliance with his orders the United States troops are now marching to the defence of the police. There is nothing further for us to do. You will therefore disperse."

And without a word, in perfect quiet and order, the crowd began to break up and move off up and down the levee. Curious as usual to see all there was to be seen, I suggested to Harrod that we should go to the station. He assented, and we elbowed our way through the crowd; reached the street that runs along the upper side of the Square from the levee to Chartres Street; found it utterly deserted, and so, rapidly pushed ahead. Presently we drew near enough to see that the head of the street was occupied by the cannon and its detachment, and a company of police. The next instant, half a dozen bayonets came flashing down upon us. We were surrounded by a squad of men under command of a darky sergeant, and with loud summons to surrender, and much excited adjuration not to resist if we didn't want want our heads blown off, Colonel Summers and myself were roughly seized and hustled towards the station.

"Here's two of the d—d scoundrels anyway," was our introduction to the men in the ranks as we were hurried along, and my very vehement protestations were lost amid the chorus of jeers with which we were greeted. Already we were within a few yards of the station-house door, when I caught sight of the aide-de-camp talking with the chief of police. I shouted his name, despite the savage order from my captors to shut my mouth if I didn't want to be killed, and instantly he recognized me, sprang forward, and ordered the police to stand back, which they sulkily did. I breathlessly introduced Colonel Summers, and he too was freed from the rude grasp of the two stalwart "peelers" who held him. Then the chief came up. Explanations followed, and despite my indignation we had a general laugh.

"My men are somewhat nervous to-night," said he, apologetically. "Even the full uniform of the captain here did not protect him, you see; the pickets up the street fired at him as he came to the rescue, but I will send a sergeant with you to see you safely through the lines." So after taking a look at the demolished station-house, we were courteously escorted up Chartres Street, and in a few minutes we were laughingly telling our adventures to the ladies on our gallery.

Even as Harrod was in the midst of the recital, there was heard the rapid tramp of many hoofs up the street, and a troop of cavalry came sweeping down at rapid trot. Well out to the front, followed by his trumpeter, rode a tall, slender young officer, whose form was now familiar to us all. He glanced up at our balcony as he passed beneath us, the moonlight shining full in his brave young face. Pauline waved her handkerchief; a gauntleted hand returned the salute; and with Kitty's eyes furtively following him Frank Amory swept by.

CHAPTER XI.

LATER in the night, after the ladies had retired, Harrod and I once more walked down to the square to see how things were going on. All was very quiet. A battalion of regular infantry had stacked its arms in the middle of the street in front of the dismantled station-house; the men were seated along the curbstone; some in their weariness were lying asleep upon the stone pavement; the officers, grouped under the archways of the old police court on the other side of the street, were puffing their cigarettes and sleepily discussing the situation. Major Williams and his command were not there; the battalion on duty was one which had been for some time past stationed at Jackson Barracks below the city. A little farther down we came upon Amory and his troop making a night of it in front of the Cathedral. The horses were still saddled, though with loosened girths, but had been unbitted, and were busily munching at the hay spread before them on the pavement. Mars himself was seated on the curbstone with a grain-sack in his lap, petting his horse's head as that quadruped blissfully devoured the oats with which his thoughtful master had heaped the sack. Harrod hailed him gleefully.

"That takes a fellow back to old times, lad, only oats were scarcer than horses."

Mars held out his unoccupied hand, looking up with rather a tired smile on his face.

"How's Vinton?" he asked.

"Very much better, we think," said Harrod, "though he is very weak, and has had an ugly siege. I think he will be housed some time yet."

"Did you see—did you happen to hear of any letter for me at Sandbrook before you came away? I told them to forward everything, but nothing has come."

"No," replied Harrod. "Had there been anything I think they would have told us, though it may be that letters were simply redirected and dropped in the Corinth mail."

There was so much anxiety in Amory's face that it suddenly occurred to me to ask, "Your mother is not ill, I hope? You have heard from her?"

"Mother is quite well, thanks. I had telegraphed her of our move, and a letter reached me yesterday. This was—I rather expected another letter." And even in the pale moonlight it was plain that Mr. Amory was blushing vividly. Instantly I was reminded of the letter he had received at camp, and received with such evident excitement. Was it from that source he now looked for another? If so, what did it mean? Mars was getting to be a mystery.

"When are you coming to see us?" asked the colonel.

"I don't know. I'd like to come at once, but you see how I'm fixed,—the only officer with the troop."

"Well, if all should be quiet to-morrow, come and dine with us at Moreau's at six, will you?" persisted Harrod. "There will be no one but ourselves and the ladies, you know; and if you are pressed for time just meet us there. We'll expect you."

"I would be delighted to," answered the young fellow, though in a strangely embarrassed and hesitating way, "but I really cannot promise. You see how it is, don't you?" he continued, looking almost appealingly at me; but I chose not to "see how it was," and only insisted on seconding Harrod's invitation. All the old Adam in me was wild with curiosity to see him with Kitty once more, and his reluctance or hesitancy was something that only served to make me more persistent. Have you never noticed that amiable trait in many a man or woman who, having passed the meridian of life him- or herself, seems bent on directing in the most trivial matters the plans and movements of younger persons? It was no earthly business of mine,

and yet I was determined to have Mars come
and see Kitty whether he wanted to or not
Harrod, of course, was actua ed by no such
motives.

Early on the following day, on going to my
office, the few letters deposited on the desk were
naturally the first things to be disposed of. Almost wearily I glanced at the superscriptions,
for nobody in New Orleans felt particularly
business-like that morning. Some were from
correspondents up the railway; others from
"down the coast." I simply glanced at their
envelopes, and had just about completed the
list, when suddenly hand and eye rested upon
a dainty little missive, an envelope of creamy
white, and addressed to me—to *me* in the very
handwriting that had so attracted my attention
and curiosity in Amory's tent at Sandbrook.
Here was the same exquisite chirography. I
knew I had seen it before. I knew now why it
seemed so familiar then. For six years or there-
abouts it had not fallen under my gaze; and
when it did, six years before, it was only that a
proud papa might exhibit to me the beautiful
writing of his daughter, then in her last year at
school in New York City, the youngest child of
a sister long since dead. It was the handwriting
of my pretty niece, Bella Grayson,—Bella, whom
I had not seen since her girlhood, and all at
once it flashed across my perturbed brain that

14*

Frank Amory's mysterious correspondent was this self-same Bella. Here was a revelation indeed!

For some minutes I was too much confounded to open the letter. Then I proceeded to read it. A very bright, graceful, well-expressed note it proved to be. Uncle George was appropriately reminded that it was more than two years since he had written to papa. Papa did not propose to write again until his letters were answered; but, feeling a trifle uneasy while reading the accounts of the stormy times in New Orleans, and having seen occasional mention of Uncle George in connection with Ku-Klux excitements, she had been commissioned to make inquiries as to Uncle George's health and fortunes, to express the hope that Uncle George would no longer neglect them as he had, and to subscribe herself very affectionately, Uncle George's niece, Bella.

So far so good. Uncle George had very vivid recollections of Miss Bella in her graduating years, and had been vastly impressed by the vivacity, wit, and sparkle of the bright little lady who made his last visit to her father's home so pleasant a thing to look back upon. From that time to this he had never seen her, but never had she been entirely dropped from his remembrance. For four years or so he had occasionally occupied himself in the metaphorical selection of an appropriate wedding-present, as home letters gave indications that Miss Bella was contemplating matrimony; but it never seemed to pass the point of contemplation. Twice at least, on authoritative announcements, Miss Bella had been "engaged." A dozen times at least, if reports were to be relied upon, Miss Bella was on the verge of that social entanglement. It was in the winter of '65 that she had first begun to exercise that involuntary gift of fascination over Uncle George which seemed to involve him, as it did all masculines who came within the sphere of her movements. I say involuntary, because then and ever afterwards, Miss Bella was wont to protest that she was no more conscious of any effort or desire to attract than she was of breathing when asleep. She had spent some months of the preceding summer and autumn at West Point. She was *petite*, graceful, not absolutely a beauty, yet there was something about those large, clear, heavily-lashed gray eyes of hers that had all the effect and power of beauty; and even when only eighteen, as she was then, Miss Bella had learned their influence, and, involuntarily of course, how to use them. I had not been a witness of the campaign itself, but I could not live in their cosey home in the city for a week without becoming measurably aware of its results. The postman's visits to the Grayson residence were as regular as his rounds, and it often happened that letters deposited on the hall-table were left there some hours, awaiting Miss Bella's return from calls or drives or strolls with her society friends of both sexes, and that I, in search of my own mail, should look over the pile on the marble slab. There was always one postmarked West Point; there was sometimes more; and there were no less than three separate and distinct handwritings thus making frequent calls at our house. In my avuncular capacity I had ventured to say something intended to be arch with regard to those letters. It was at the breakfast-table. Miss Bella was pouring coffee, and doing it with a deft and graceful turn of the wrist that showed her slender white hand to vast advantage. For all answer she had given me one of those searching glances from under the deep lids; looked me squarely in the face, though a merry smile was hovering about the corners of her rosy mouth; and, neither admitting nor denying the correspondence, had disarmed me by a prompt inquiry as to whether I really thought it improper for her to hear from her cadet friends.

No one could ever call it a correspondence, for no one ever saw Miss Bella writing, or heard of her mailing letters to West Point or anywhere else. Between her and her devoted papa the closest sympathy and alliance existed. He seemed to take a jovial delight in Bella's fascinations. She ruled him with a winning and imperious sway that was delicious to see, and Uncle George speedily fell into the same groove, with this difference: she may have told her father who her correspondents were; she never did tell Uncle George. What was more, Uncle George never could find out. Despite several efforts to win the young lady's confidence in his somewhat bulky and blundering way, Uncle George had had to give it up. She was impenetrable as a sphinx.

And now, six years afterwards, here she reappeared in his life; and, if Uncle George was not very much mistaken, Miss Bella was the correspondent whose letter had caused Frank Amory so much excitement and emotion that last day in camp at Sandbrook. It was her letter he was so eagerly awaiting now. And all this time——

Well. To the neglect of other letters I sat at the desk pondering over this maidenly missive; then with an effort refolded and was about to close it, when my eyes were attracted by some lines on the outer page. Who was it who first said that the gist of a woman's letter would always be found in the postscript? There, on page four of the tiny note-sheet, were the words:

"P. S.—So you have met Mr. Amory of the cavalry, and you had quite an exciting adventure, too. Should you see him again pray remember me to him, though it is quite possible he has forgotten me. We were good friends during his 'first class camp.'"

Oh, Bella Grayson! "Pray remember me to him," indeed! "Quite possible he has forgotten me." Upon my word, young lady, this is too much even for a long-suffering uncle. Asking me to remember her to a young fellow with whom she was actually in correspondence at the time! For a moment I was fairly indignant; but something of the witchery of Bella's own caressing voice and manner seemed to steal from the folds of the tiny note. A dozen things that had been told me of her from time to time came floating back to my brain, and—I couldn't help it—I began to laugh.

Once, just before his coming South, Miss Bella had appeared before Uncle George in a state of indignation. A young man whom he rather liked had been one of her devotees for a month or more, and then suddenly ceased his attentions. Bella's eyes flashed as she half reluctantly related to Uncle George (in response to his urgent request) the circumstances which led to the sudden break. "He dared to say to me that, if no more attractive subject happened to be available, it was his belief I would flirt with a chimney-sweep!" and then, when Uncle George burst into a fit of uncontrollable merriment, Miss Bella had first flushed with indignation, then her irresistible sense of the humorous began to get the better of her resolution to be deeply offended, and presently she laughed too; laughed till the tears ran down her cheeks; laughed as only Bella could laugh, the most musical, ringing, delightful laugh ever heard; and then, suddenly recollecting herself, she had pronounced Uncle George an unfeeling wretch, and flounced out of the room in high dudgeon.

Now, it is contrary to all principles of story-telling to introduce an utterly new character towards the fag end of a narrative, but Mr. Brandon makes no pretensions to being a story-teller. He can only relate things as they happened; and never, until this stage of the game, had his fair niece Bella appeared as a factor in the plot so far as his knowledge went. Nevertheless, it was vividly apparent to Mr. Brandon that now at least she was destined to become a leading lady, a power behind the throne, whether she appeared in person upon the boards or not. He recalled the frequent allusions to her in the letters that used to reach him from the North in the days when he found time to keep up correspondence with the scattered family. There was a tone of almost tragic despair in the letters of one of her aunts whenever Bella was the subject under discussion. Wherever she went—and she went pretty much everywhere—Miss Grayson was the centre of a knot of admirers. Her summers were spent at West Point or on "the Sound;" her winters in New York or Syracuse; and the oddest thing about it all was that, despite her great attractiveness among the beaus of society, she retained an absolute dominion over the hearts of a little coterie of schoolmates, —a sextette of as bright and intelligent and attractive girls as Uncle George had ever seen; two of them undoubted beauties; all of them gracious and winning; yet, as though by common and tacit understanding, when Bella appeared in their midst, and the men concentrated their attentions upon her, the others contentedly, even approvingly, so it seemed, fell into the background. They had their own personal worshippers, to be sure, but they were paraded for Bella's inspection and approval before being decided upon. Two of the sisterhood married within a few years of their graduation after receiving Bella's sanction. It had even been alleged that, involuntarily as usual, Bella had diverted the growing admiration of one youth from a sister to herself; but the unruffled sweetness of the sisterly relations seemed to give the lie to that statement.

But Bella's fascinations were not so placidly accepted with the opposite sex. It had been a pet theory of hers that cadets and officers were fair game for flirtation *à l'outrance*. She had become involved in her very first visit to the

Academy in two very serious affairs; retaining
complete mastery over her own susceptibilities,
while obtaining mastery as complete over those
of two cadet admirers who chanced to be rather
close friends. One of them, at least, had been
desperately in earnest at the outset; both of them
were before they got through; and Bella was,
or professed to be, totally incapable of believing
that they had intended more than a mere flirtation. To her credit be it said, she was grievously distressed when the actual truth came to
light; but her theories were in nowise shaken,
for with the following year a still more desperate
victim was at her feet, while the singed moths
of the previous season looked gloomily and sar-
donically on the throes which they had so recently suffered. It was an attribute of Bella's
as marvellous as the ascendency she maintained
over her sisterhood, that even in jilting an admirer she had so sweet, sympathetic, caressing,
and self-reproachful a manner as to make the
poor devil feel that the whole thing was his own
fault, or that of his blindness; and to send him
on his way comforted, perhaps enslaved. She
never could succeed in absolutely and definitely
disposing of a lover. New ones might come,
and did come, every season of the year. She
had them wherever she moved; but Bella could
no more let one go than a cat could a captured
mouse,—another statement at her expense that

first excited her wrath and afterwards nearly convulsed her by its humorous accuracy. She would turn her back on him; lose sight of him to all appearances; but let him but display a desire for freedom; let him but make an effort to get away from the toils; and under the *patte de velours* was an inflexible grasp that once more stretched the victim panting at her feet.

And yet she was so winning, so plaintive, so appealing with it all! Volumes of pity and trust and sympathy beamed from Bella's clear gray eyes. Volumes of half-playful reproach and condolence in the letters she would write. "Even in bidding you go she implores you to stay," was once said of her by an exasperated yet enthralled victim, and Uncle George was quite ready to believe it.

And Bella was still unmarried; still careering over the old preserves; still maintaining, apparently, her old theory that "men are deceivers ever;" and still, to judge from recent developments, bringing down fresh victims among the too inflammable youngsters of the battalion of cadets. Now, was Frank Amory a victim in good earnest, or only a narrow escape from being one? She wrote to him, but that proved nothing: she wrote to a dozen, and all at the same time. Aunt Ethel declared of her that she was writing to two classmates an entire winter, receiving almost daily missives from both, and responding when she felt disposed; and that not until they came to be stationed at the same post; to occupy the same quarters; to make the simultaneous discovery that each had parted with his class ring; and, one never-to-be-forgotten day, that each was receiving letters from the same damsel; had either of the young fellows the faintest idea that he was not the sole possessor of such attentions. It was alleged of Bella that she could have worn a class ring on every finger if she chose; but whatever may have been her object in accepting them, it was not for purposes of self-glorification. Her most intimate friend never knew whose rings she had; never knew how many; and Bella's flirtations, whatever may have been the wide-spread destruction she effected, were subjects that never could be spoken of in her presence. A dozen men were believed to confide in her, and she held their confidence inviolable. No one of them ever extracted from her the faintest admission that she ever received a line or an attention from any one else.

Now, what in the world was I to do? Here was a complication that baffled me completely. If Mars were really smitten with my fascinating niece, how far had it gone? That he had been I could readily believe; but, whether she looked it or not, Bella must now be older than he, and probably had only been—involuntarily, as usual—amusing herself with his devotions. And now he was interested in Kitty,—of that I felt certain,—and, by Jove! I had it. He felt himself still bound by the old ties; still fettered by some real or imaginary allegiance to his West Point affinity; still—"Why, the whole thing was plain as A, B, C," thought I, in my masculine profundity. "Bella would not accept, could not discard him, and here she has kept him dangling at her beck and call ever since." I decided to write to Bella,—oh, the bewildering idiocy of some men!—and I wrote forthwith.

That evening a letter winding up as follows was on its way northward:

"Yes, I have met your friend, young Amory; have seen a good deal of him, in fact, and am greatly interested in him. He strikes me as a gallant young soldier and gentleman, and his evident admiration for a fair young friend of mine—an heiress, by the way—commands my entire sympathy. I've half a mind to take you into my confidence, Bella, for perhaps you can dispel my perplexity. I *think*—mind you, I only say I *think*—that the young people are quite ready to fall in love with one another. They have been thrown together under most romantic circumstances, but he has behaved very oddly of late, and I could not but indulge in some theory as to the cause. I have learned that he has some young lady correspondent up North, and, knowing what susceptible fellows cadets are (from your own statements), it has occurred to me that he may have gotten into some entanglement there from which he would now gladly escape. Now, Bella, put on your thinking-cap. You have been there every summer for six or eight years (oh!), and although much above cadets now I fancy, you still retain your old ascendency over the sex. You knew Amory well, probably, and possibly he has made you a confidante of his affairs. What young girl was there to whom he was devoted? Perhaps you and I can help him out of his boyish folly and into something that is worth having."

Was there *ever* such a colossal ass?

CHAPTER XII.

THAT evening we dined at Moreau's. Things had quieted down in the city, though the troops still remained on duty in the streets; and it was with eager anticipation of meeting Frank Amory that I wended my way to the tidy old restaurant with its sanded floor, its glittering array of little tables, and the ever-attentive waiters. Colonel Summers and his party had not yet arrived. Would Monsieur step up to the room and wait their coming? Monsieur would; and, taking the *Evening Picayune* to while away the time, Mr. Brandon seated himself on the balcony overlooking Canal Street,—busy, bustling, thronged as usual; yet bustling in the languid, Latinized sense of the term; bustling in a way too unlike our Northern business centres to justify the use of the term. No sign of disorder or turmoil was manifest. The banquettes on both sides were covered with ladies and children; the street-cars on the esplanade were filled with passengers going in every direction; the booths, fruit-stands, confectioneries were all doing a thriving business; the newsboys were scurrying to and fro in their picturesque tatters screaming the head-lines of their evening bulletins; carriages and cabriolets were rattling to and fro; the setting sun shone hot on the glaring façade of the stone Custom-House down the street; and beyond, across the crowded and dusty levee, dense volumes of black smoke were rising from the towering chimneys of the boats even now pushing from the shore and ploughing huskily up the stream. All spoke of business activity and lively trade. The mercurial spirit of the populace seemed to have subsided to the normal level; and the riot of yesterday was a thing of the distant past.

Voices on the stairs called me into the cosey room, and Kitty entered radiant; with her—not Mars but Mr. Turpin; behind her, Colonel Summers and the doctor. Pauline had again decided to remain and take tea with the landlady, but Vinton was improving, said Harrod, who instantly added an inquiry for Amory.

"He has not been here, nor have I seen him to-day. Have you, Mr. Turpin?" I asked.

"No, sir. Amory and his troop were sent up to Jeffersonville at noon, so I learned at headquarters, and they have not come back since."

"Then we must go on without him," said Harrod, and dinner was ordered forthwith.

Seated by Kitty's side, Mr. Turpin was soon absorbed in the duty of making himself agreeable. Evidently they had been talking of Amory before coming in, and, whether piqued at the latter's conduct in not yet having been to see her, or worse, at his having been there to inquire for Vinton and not for her, Kitty was in the very mood to render her new admirer's attentions acceptable. She was sparkling with animation. She was listening with flattering eagerness to everything he said, laughing merrily at every sally; urging him to tell more of his cadet days and army life; paying no heed to any of the rest of us; plainly, only too plainly, bent on fascinating her infantry friend, and fascination it plainly was. Mr. Turpin was head over heels in love with her before dinner was half over; and while we oldsters were discussing our cigars and *pousse café* on the balcony after that repast, they were seated on the sofa merrily, intently chatting together, as firm friends as though they had known one another from childhood. So intent that my entrance for a match in nowise disturbed them; so utterly intent that they never saw what I saw at once,— Frank Amory standing at the door.

To my eager welcome he responded absently. Turpin sprang up and held out his hand, which was taken in a perfunctory sort of way, but there was no heartiness in his reply to the cordial greeting of his classmate. He bowed in a constrained manner to Kitty, who had flushed with surprise—possibly some other emotion—when she caught sight of him; and then without further notice of either her or her companion, he passed on to where Harrod was standing at the open window, and eagerly inquired for Vinton, but his bearing was forced and unnatural. He had already dined, he said, and had been unable to get back from Jeffersonville with the troop until late, too late to accept Colonel Summers's invitation; so he had merely dropped in to inquire after his captain, as he thought we would still be here; and now, he said, he must hasten to the warehouse on Magazine Street, as there was no telling how soon he and his men might be needed again. We urged him to stay and make one of a party to go to the theatre, but Mars was adamant. His refusal was even curt. "Pray make my excuses and apologies to the ladies. *I'll* go down through the hall," were his parting words. And so, without even having touched Kitty's hand or spoken a sentence to her by way of welcome, Mr. Amory took his leave.

Was he "miffed" because he had found Turpin in happy *tête-à-tête* with her? Had he hoped to reserve that happiness to himself; or was there some deeper reason to account for his avoidance of her? Kitty evidently adopted the first-mentioned explanation of his conduct; ascribed his cold salutation and sudden departure to jealousy,

m

—absolute jealousy,—and I am bound to say that so far from being depressed or saddened by his conduct she seemed to derive additional inspiration or stimulant. A burning color had mounted to her cheeks; her eyes had taken an almost defiant sparkle; her coquetry with Turpin became more marked than before; and, as though elated at the betrayal of Amory's feelings, and excited by the exhibition of his jealousy, she seemed in extraordinary spirits. Turpin promptly accepted the invitation to go to the theatre, provided he could obtain Major Williams's permission to be absent from the battalion during the evening, and went off to see about it forthwith, agreeing to join us at the Royal Street lodgings in fifteen minutes. In less than fifteen minutes we were there. Kitty ran blithely up-stairs to see Pauline, and then Harrod turned to me.

"Brandon, did you notice anything wrong with Amory to-night?" he asked, anxiously.

"He was excited, perhaps upset, at seeing Turpin where he was; but why do you ask?"

"It was something more than that, I fear. Did you notice his eyes, his color? Did you feel his hand?"

"He was flushed, I noticed, and I thought it due to riding all day in the sun; but his hand I did not touch."

"It was burning as though with fever. Can

he have been seized as Vinton was?" said the colonel. And for a moment we looked at one another in silence. "You know he has been up and around now for several nights, and exposed all day to the heat of the sun. The extremes are dangerous to those not accustomed to our Louisiana climate, and if he had contracted any disorder this would bring it out. Here comes Mr. Turpin," continued the colonel. "Let us ask him what he observed."

Turpin joined us with his quick, springy step. "The major says I may go," he spoke blithely; "but is not Amory coming?"

"It was of Amory we wanted to ask you," said Harrod. "He seemed very unlike himself the few minutes he was at Moreau's. Did you note anything out of the way?"

Turpin flushed. "Why—yes," said he, hesitatingly. "He seemed a little queer—a good deal stiff and formal and——"

"But as to his health. Do you think he is well?"

"Why," said Turpin, with a sudden start, "I had not thought of that. I ascribed his manner to—to—well, he always was a quick, impulsive fellow, and I thought perhaps he regarded me as being in the way; but his hand *was* hot,—hot as fire. I'm ashamed I did not think of it before."

And then he stopped short, for Kitty re-entered. She walked smilingly up to Mr. Turpin with extended hand.

"You can go?" she said. "I'm so glad. How soon must we start? Pauline is coming down a moment." And with Pauline's coming we forgot for the time being our talk about Amory.

Very gentle, very lovely, looked Miss Summers as she stood answering our warm inquiries about the major. He was so much better; was sleeping quietly and naturally, the nurse said; and the doctor was so delighted with the improvement, and had let her sit for a while by the bedside and talk to him, though the major himself was forbidden to talk. She was *so* glad we were going to the theatre. It must be wearisome staying around the house for us, though she could not bear to go. And so we bade her goodnight and went on our way.

The Varieties was crowded that night, and an admirable play was on the stage; but my thoughts were incessantly wandering back to Mars, to his strange behavior, and to Bella Grayson and her possible connection with his changed manner. Then, too, I was worried about Harrod's theory,— that the boy was ill. All things considered, I could pay very little attention to what was going on, either in the audience or on the stage. Our seats were in the front row of the dress-circle, a little to the right of the centre of the house; and during the intermission between the first and second acts Kitty and Turpin had been keeping up an incessant chatter, though so low-toned and semi-confidential that I heard nothing of what was said. The house was very full, as I say, and many gentlemen were standing in the side aisles over the proscenium boxes. Others were swarming about the outer row of dress-circle seats. Others still were seated on the steps leading down into the parquet. The curtain rose upon the second act, and Kitty, sitting next to me, with Turpin on her other side, drew back and glanced one minute up in my face. All animation, life, sparkle, and saucy triumph she looked; there was a mischievous challenge in her laughing eyes as they met mine, then wandered off to the stage. Another moment and I turned to her to whisper some comment upon the costume worn by one of the actresses and—how can I describe the change that had come over her face? Pale, startled, yes, frightened. She was staring across the parquet towards a group of men standing in the outer aisle. Following her eyes I too looked, and there, glaring at our party, with a strange, wild, uncanny expression on his face, was Frank Amory.

For an instant nothing was said. Then, involuntarily, I half rose. His eyes met mine, and, without a sign of recognition, he dropped back in the throng and disappeared. "Did you see him?" I exclaimed to Harrod. "Watch! See where he goes! It is Amory, and something is wrong."

The colonel looked at me in startled wonderment, but a glance at Kitty's face seemed to bring him confirmation of my statement. I rose and looked about in my excitement and anxiety, but an indignant " Down in front!" from some half-dozen mouths in rear brought me back to seat and senses. Not until the close of the act could I get out. Then, followed by Harrod, I worked my way into the vestibule, searched the corridors, the bar-room, the main stairway, and the broad entrance. No sign of him. Several infantry officers were standing there, but, in answer to my appeal, said they had seen nothing of Lieutenant Amory; but at the gate the door-keeper remembered a young officer going out in the middle of the second act and declining a return check. I determined to go at once to his lodgings. Harrod would stay and look after Kitty and Turpin.

In half an hour I had reached the warehouse. A sleepy sentinel told me that the lieutenant was not there. He occupied a room "over beyant," in a large frame boarding-house. Ringing the bell, a colored servant answered. Would he show me to Lieutenant Amory's room? He would, and we went up the main stairway and out on a back gallery to one of those little ten by six boxes, without which no New Orleans boarding-place is complete. No answer to our knock, but the door was unlocked, and I entered and turned up the light. There stood his trunk, open. Papers and letters were strewn on the bureau, and among them, almost the first to catch my eye, was a dainty envelope addressed in that graceful, unmistakable hand to Lieutenant Frank Amory at Sandbrook, and forwarded thence to New Orleans. He had had another letter, then, from Bella.

In answer to inquiries, the servant said that Mr. Amory had come in "lookin' mighty tired" late in the afternoon; had taken a bath, dressed, and gone out again without saying a word to anybody, and had not been back since. Telling him he might go, I decided to await Amory's return. I knew not where to search for him.

It was then late. The bells of the churches over on Camp Street and Lafayette Square were chiming ten o'clock. All below was very quiet. The distant roar of wheels down towards Canal Street, and the tinkle of the mule-cars were the only sounds that struck upon the ear. I felt strangely worried and depressed, and sought for something with which to occupy my thoughts and keep me from brooding. Books there were none, for Mars had had no time for reading since his arrival; paper, envelopes, some open letters were on the bureau with her envelope, but the letter it had contained was gone. Tossing them over with impatient hand, I came upon two envelopes addressed in his vigorous hand; one to his mother, the other to Miss Isabel R. Grayson, care of Hon. H. C. Grayson, Syracuse, New York,— further confirmation of my theory. Then there were some scraps of paper on which he had been scribbling; and on one, written perhaps a dozen times, was the name "Kittie." That was his way, then, of spelling it.

An hour passed by. Eleven o'clock came, and no Amory. I could stand it no longer. Once more I went out on Magazine Street, and over to the warehouse. This time a corporal of the guard met me and seemed to know me.

"No, sir. The lieutenant hasn't been in all night, sir, and it isn't his way at all. He may be over at headquarters. Shall I send, sir?"

No. I decided to go myself.

Late as it was, a broad glare of light shone out from the upper windows of the handsome brownstone residence, occupied at the time by the commanding general as the offices of himself and the staff. The lower hall was open. I entered and went up-stairs to the first open door. One or two officers in undress uniform were lounging about; and, seeing me, Colonel Newhall sprang up and came hastily forward, inviting me to enter. I inquired at once for Amory, and briefly stated that we feared he was not well. This brought to his feet the junior aide-de-camp whom we had seen galloping down Chartres Street the previous night.

"Amory was here early in the evening asking for me," he said, "and he left this note. I cannot understand. He seems worried about something."

I took the note and read,—

"DEAR PARKER: Both times I've been in to see you to-day, you happened to be out. I *must* see you. I must get a leave and go North at once. Can you suggest any way of helping me? Some one must take the troop. I'll be in this evening. Do wait for me.

"Yours,
"AMORY."

"It is after eleven now and no sign of him," said the aide. "You say you thought he looked ill?"

"Very ill," I answered, "and I am strangely worried."

"Sit down just a few minutes until I see the general. Then, if possible, I'll go with you and see if we can find him."

Perhaps ten minutes afterwards we were on our way back to his temporary quarters, when the aide-de-camp called out to a man whom I saw hurrying along the opposite side of the street under the gas-lamp, and the very corporal who was on duty at the stables came springing over the cobble-stones.

"I was looking for you, sir," he said, breathlessly. "Did you see the lieutenant?"

"No; where is he?"

"I don't know, sir. Directly after you left he jumped off a street-car and ordered us to saddle up. I routed out the first sergeant and the men, but before they could get their clothes and belts on he had leaped on his horse and galloped off down the street like mad. We don't know what to do, sir."

"Which way did he go?" quickly asked the officer with me.

"Down the street, sir, towards Canal."

"Give me one of your fastest horses. Tell the first sergeant I want to see him at once, and let the men unsaddle again."

"What do you think it is?" I anxiously asked.

"Fever; and he is twice as delirious as Vinton was. We must find him at once."

CHAPTER XIII.

THAT night we had a chase such as I had never before indulged in. The aide-de-camp believed Frank Amory to be ill with fever:—delirium in fact, but to my knowledge delirium was unusual as a first symptom of an ordinary Southern fever. He might be feverish; might indeed be ill; but that alone would not be apt to cause his extraordinary excitement. Two or three officers at headquarters had remarked his strange manner and absent-minded replies, said the aide, while he had been there early in the evening, but at that time his face was pale rather than flushed.

At the stables on Magazine Street we again questioned the sergeant. "Did the lieutenant appear to be under any strong excitement?" asked the aide-de-camp, and the sergeant eyed him askance a moment as though he misunderstood the drift of the question, seeing which I interposed,—

"The captain fears that Mr. Amory is seized with just such a fever as that which prostrated Major Vinton." Whereat the sergeant looked relieved, and answered,—

"I couldn't say, sir. He never spoke more

than to order his horse and then go off at a gallop. But two or three times lately at Sandbrook he has done that,—taken his horse and gone off riding at the dead of night. He may be ill, sir, but I couldn't say."

This news in some way strengthened my view of the case. The fact that he had frequently or occasionally gone off in a similar manner went to prove that the ailment was not a new bodily trouble. Knowing what I knew and felt bound to keep to myself, it was not hard to determine that mental perturbations, aggravated perhaps by recent fatigues and excitements, were at the bottom of Amory's strange conduct. None the less, however, I was eager to find and bring him back. He ought not to be away from his command at such a time. Directing the sergeant to say to Mr. Amory that we were in search of him and begged him to wait for us on his return, the aide-de-camp and I hurried down the street; sought a cab-stand; and, jumping into one of the light cabriolets that were then a feature of the New Orleans streets, we drove rapidly down to Vinton's quarters. I thought Amory might have galloped thither. A dim light was burning in the sick-room, as we could see from the front. The door was closed and locked, but I rang, and presently a servant came sleepily through the hall and stared at me in mild stupefaction. "No. Mr. Amory hadn't been there."

I brushed past the darky and went noiselessly up the stairs and tapped at Vinton's door. The nurse came and peered at me through the inch-wide crack; not a whit more would he open the door lest the night air should be wafted in.

"We fear that Lieutenant Amory is taken ill," I said in a low tone. "He may come here to see his captain. Try and get him to lie down in Colonel Summers's room until we get back, if he should come." The nurse nodded; said that Vinton was sleeping quietly, and directed me to Harrod's door. I knocked there, and it was opened in a moment.

"What! you, Brandon? Anything wrong?"

"We can't find Amory. He is on horseback and galloping around town all by himself. They think at headquarters that he may be ill with fever like Vinton. Mr. Parker and I are hunting for him. If he should come here, get him into your room and make him lie down, will you?"

"Certainly I will. But, Brandon, had not I better go with you? Are you sure he is ill? I thought him strange enough at Moreau's,

I broke in, impa-
he must be found

and retraced my
hall. Reaching

the stairs I paused, for another door had softly opened, and Pauline's voice, low-toned and anxious, was heard.

"Harrod, what is it?"

"Mr. Amory is ill, I'm afraid," was the reply, and I hurried back to the street.

Rapidly we drove to the levee, and there at the depot found Major Williams's sleeping battalion. The aide sprang out and accosted a sentry. A sergeant came with a lantern and ushered the staff-officer in among the snoring groups; for the men had thrown themselves in their blankets upon the wooden flooring. Presently they reappeared, and with them came Mr. Turpin, hurriedly adjusting his collar and cravat.

"Sheep always was a most excitable fellow," he was saying, "but this beats me. He hasn't been here at all, and I've no idea where he can have gone."

Leaving directions what was to be done in case he did appear, we drove away up Canal Street. It was then nearly two o'clock, but there were still loungers around the Clay statue; lights gleaming from one or two "open-all-night" bars and from the cab-lanterns on St. Charles Street. Our driver pulled up, and Mr. Parker sprang out and exchanged a few words with a policeman. I could not hear, but saw that the latter pointed up the street; and the aide came quickly back,—

"Drive on,—right out Canal, and keep a bright lookout for an officer on horseback," were his orders, as we whirled away over the smooth pavement.

"That policeman says he saw a young officer gallop out this way not ten minutes ago, and he's been wondering ever since what was going on. He walked up as far as Dryades Street to find out, thinking he might have stopped at the State-House; but all is quiet there, and the patrols told him the officer went on out Canal, riding like mad."

Evidently, then, Mars had stopped somewhere or had ridden elsewhere before going out towards the swamps. We peered eagerly up and down the dimly-lighted cross-streets as we whirled rapidly past them. The lamps along the broad thoroughfare grew infrequent; the street was deserted. Once in a while we passed a carriage-load of revellers returning from the shell road and a supper at the "Lake End." Well out towards the stables of the street-railway we caught sight of another policeman; hauled up, and hailed him with anxious questioning. No, he had seen no officer on horseback; his beat lay along Canal Street, but he had "taken a turn through a side street after a couple of s'picious-lookin' parties," and might have been gone four or five minutes. Crack! went the whip, and we pushed ahead. Gas-lamps now became few and far between; open stretches of level turf or prairie were visible here and there between the houses or garden-walls; the moonlight was tempered and shrouded by low-hanging clouds, and surrounding objects were only dimly seen. Still we whirled ahead over the smooth-beaten road, and at last drove rapidly between the high walls of the silent cities of the dead that bounded the highway near the crossing of the canal. Two or three loungers were hanging about the dimly-lighted portico of a saloon. Mr. Parker sprang out and made some rapid inquiries, then hurried back to the cab.

"He crossed here nearly half an hour ago,— went right on over the bridge," he exclaimed, as he sprang in and told the driver to whip up. "Turn to the right," he added. "Drive towards Lake End. It's the only place he can have gone." And in a moment more the wheels were whirring over the level track; a dense hedgerow of swamp undergrowth on our left; the dark waters of the canal on our right.

We passed two or three roadside hostelries, whose enticing lights still lured the belated or the dissipated into the ready bars. Mr. Parker scanned them as we drove ahead.

"He never drinks a drop, I hear, and it's no use looking for him there."

Nevertheless, our driver suddenly pulled up in front of a lamp-lighted entrance. "There's a couple of buggies and a horse in under that shed," said he.

The aide-de-camp jumped out and stepped briskly off in the direction indicated by the driver's hand. Our cab again pulled up. Presently he emerged from the darkness of the shed.

"It isn't Amory's horse. It's a Louisiana pony," said he. "Wait one moment and I'll see who's inside."

With that he sprang up the steps and walked rapidly towards the glass doorways of the bar.

He was in civilian dress except for the forage-cap, which he had hastily picked up when we left the office. Its gold cord and crossed sabres gleamed under the lamp as he sharply turned the door-knob and entered the room. Even without that cap I by this time would have known his profession; he had that quick, springy, nervous walk and erect carriage so marked among the younger West-Pointers. My eyes followed him until he disappeared; so apparently did others.

From the farther end of the gallery two dark forms rose from a sitting posture, and one of them came tiptoeing along towards the doorway. Our cab had halted near the steps at the end opposite them, and, despite our lights, the stealthily-moving figure seemed to pay no attention to us. Before I had time to conjecture what his object could be, the man crouched before the door, his hat pulled low over his forehead, and peered eagerly through the glass. Then he turned his head; gave a low whistle, and, almost at a run, the second figure, in slouch hat like the first and with overcoat pulled well up about his ears, hurried to his side; stooped; peered through, and shook his head.

"Drive up there, quick!" I said. And, as hoof and wheel crunched through the gravel, the pair drew suddenly back; sprang noiselessly down the steps and in among the shrubbery out of my sight. Almost at the same instant Mr. Parker reappeared; took his seat beside me, and, before I could interpose, called out, "Drive on,—Lake End." And away we went, leaving the mysterious strangers in the dusk behind us.

"Amory has not been seen there, nor beyond. There are two young sports in there who came in from Lake End half an hour ago, but they are both pretty full. The barkeeper said there were two more gentlemen who came out from town with another buggy earlier, but they had gone outside."

"I saw them," answered I, "and they are bad characters of some kind. They stole up on tiptoe and peered after you as you went in, then sprang back out of sight as you came out. I wanted to tell you about them. They seemed waiting or watching for somebody."

"Gamblers or 'cappers' probably. Fellows

who lie in wait for drunken men with money and steer them into their dens,—fleece them, you know. The streets are full of them day and night."

"Yes; but these men wore slouch hats and overcoats that muffled their faces, and they watched you so oddly. Why did they leap back as you came out?"

"That was odd," said Mr. Parker, thoughtfully. "Could you see nothing of their faces?"

"Nothing at all, except that the first man had a heavy dark moustache, and was tall and stoutly built; the other seemed young and slight; his face was hidden entirely."

The aide-de-camp leaned out and looked back along the dark road; then drew in again.

"No use to look," he said. "Even if they were to follow I could not see; their buggy has no lamps, our rig has to have them. Are you armed?"

"No; I never carry anything."

"Nor I, as a rule; yet had I thought we would come so far at this time of night I would have brought my revolver. Not that any attack is to be feared from those two unless there should be a crowd at their back; otherwise we would be three to two."

"But they are armed, and we are not."

"They think we are, all the same. The average citizen hereabouts goes prepared to shoot if he is on a night-prowl like this. I don't know why I asked if you were armed."

Then for some distance we rattled along in silence. The clouds had grown heavier; a few heavy rain-drops had pattered in on our faces, and the night air was damp and raw. We passed one or two more dark houses, and then came in view of the lights at Lake End. Here, despite the lateness of the hour, one or two resorts seemed still to be open and patronized. Directing the driver to turn towards the lights on the right, Mr. Parker again sprang out, looked in the carriage-shed, then into the bar-room; came out, crossed the way, and made a similar search in a neighboring establishment. Then I saw him questioning a sleepy-looking stableman, and then he came back to me. Perplexity and concern were mingled in his face as he stood there looking up at me in the glare of our lamp.

"Nobody has been here on horseback since midnight. These are the only places open since that hour, and now there are not more than half a dozen people out here—roysterers after a late supper. Where could Amory have gone? Do you suppose he knew his way back by Washington Avenue, and had turned to the left instead of this way?"

"He is an entire stranger in New Orleans,— never was out here before in his life,—and I don't know what to make of it."

He looked at his watch, retook his seat. "We must get back to the bridge," said he. "Driver, stop at Gaston's,—where we were before,—and go lively."

Now through the pattering rain we hurried on our return trip. We were silent, plunged in thought and anxiety. In some way those two skulkers at Gaston's had become connected in my mind with Amory's disappearance. I could not shake off the impression, and, as though the same train of thought were affecting my companion, he suddenly spoke,—

"You say that those men followed me as I went in, and sprang out into the shrubbery as I came back?"

"Yes; as though to avoid being seen by you."

He took off his forage-cap and looked disgustedly at it a moment.

"Confound this thing! Why didn't I wear my hat?" he muttered; then turned suddenly to me: "Mr. Brandon, when we get back to Gaston's let me have your hat, will you? I would like to take another look in there, and if you will stay in the cab, we will stop this side of the entrance, and I'll go ahead on foot. Here, driver, hold up a moment."

Cabby reined in his horse and turned towards us in surprise. The aide-de-camp sprang out in the rain and began working at the lamp.

"Don't put it out, sir; it's against orders," said the driver.

"Never you mind, driver; I'll be responsible for any row there may be over it. There is reason for it, and a mighty good one. Douse that glim on your side. That's right! Now go ahead, lively as you can, and stop just this side of Gaston's."

Then for a while we pushed on in the darkness, and nobody spoke. Finally the driver turned, saying that Gaston's lights were near at hand; presently he reined up. Mr. Parker exchanged head-gear with me; pulled the brim of my roomy black felt well down over his face; and, cautioning us in a low tone to remain where we were, disappeared in the direction of the lights.

It must have been long after three. I was tired and chilled. The driver got out his gum coat and buttoned it around him. Five—ten minutes we waited. No sound but the dismal patter of the rain. Full quarter of an hour passed, it seemed to me, before I saw a lantern coming rapidly out of the darkness in front, and presently Mr. Parker's voice was heard.

"Come on; drive slowly. Go right in to Gaston's," and, even as he spoke, he swung in beside me. "Had Amory any money, do you know?" he asked, before fairly taking his seat.

"No. Why?"

"There is something strange about this affair I cannot fathom. I've been talking with Gaston and one of his men. They have been sitting up waiting for us to get back. Those two footpads *were* up to some mischief, and I'm afraid it was Amory they were after. You will hear in a moment. Come into the bar," he said, as the cab stopped at the steps.

Another moment and Gaston himself had ushered us into a little room and proceeded to tell his tale. We had no sooner left, he said, than those gentlemen who came from town in the buggy after midnight re-entered the bar, ordered drinks, and asked Gaston to join them. One was a big man, with a heavy moustache, and deep-set eyes under very shaggy brows; he was rather poorly dressed, and had no watch. The other was a young, dark-eyed, handsome fellow, with dark moustache, stylish clothes, and a fine gold watch, which he kept nervously looking at every moment or so. The former did all the talking; the latter paid for everything they ordered both before and after our visit. After a few ordinary remarks the big man asked Gaston who the young officer was, and Gaston, knowing him to be stationed in the city and having often seen him, gave his name. Then they wanted to know who was with him in the cab, and "what took him off so sudden." Gaston had seen nobody with him, but told them unhesitatingly that Mr. Parker was in search of a friend,—an officer who had ridden out on horseback. At this the men had looked suddenly at one another, and very soon after had gone out, saying they believed they would drive back, it looked like rain.

Five minutes afterwards, Louis, the hostler, came into the bar and asked Gaston who those men were, and, on being told that they were strangers, had replied, "Well, they're here for no good, and I'd like to follow them up. They didn't see me out there in the dark, and were talking very low and fast when they came for their buggy." We called Louis in and had his story from his own lips. He had heard their talk, and it alarmed and puzzled him. The big man was saying with an oath that some man they were waiting for must be around there somewhere; he had come across the bridge, for Gaston told them the officer said so. The little man was excited, and had answered, "Well, we've got to tackle him; but don't you drive into any light." With that and some more talk they had got into the buggy and had driven rapidly off towards the Canal Street bridge.

"How long ago?" asked Mr. Parker.

"Full half an hour," was the answer.

"Then we had better start at once," said the aide to me. "What other places are there near here that would be open now, Gaston?"

"None at all. I'd have been shut long ago but for this affair. There are one or two saloons near the bridge and the Metairie track, but none would be open this late."

Thanking them for their information, and promising to let them know if anything resulted, we hurried out to the cab and told the driver to go to the bridge. We were both more than anxious by this time, and were unable to account for the strange proceedings in any satisfactory manner.

The rain seemed to have held up for a few moments, and the veil of clouds thrown over the face of the moon had perceptibly thinned, so that a faint, wan light fell upon roadway, swamp, and canal. The lamps at the crossing burned with a yellowish glare. No one was visible around the bridge or the buildings at the city end,—no one from whom we could obtain information as to the movements of Amory or of the two strangers.

"There are one or two places over here on the upper side I mean to have a look at," said Mr. Parker, "and if no one is there, Amory must have gone back to town."

We had turned to the right, towards Lake Pontchartrain, on coming out. Now the driver was directed to go to the other side. Parker kept peering out into the darkness, and presently the driver said,—

"I think there's a light in there at Gaffney's."

"Hold up, then," said the aide. "Now, Mr.

Brandon, lend me your hat again : I'm going to hunt through one or two sheds hereabouts for that buggy. I may be gone ten or twelve minutes. You get the cab into this little side alley here and wait. Those men will be on the watch for our lamps if they are still here, but I can crawl up on them by keeping the cab out of sight."

The side alley proved to be a lane leading through the tall hedge of swampy vegetation. I could not see where it led to, but the driver said it only ran out a few hundred feet to some barns that lay near the old Metairie track. He drove in, however, and halted the cab close under the hedge on one side. Too nervous to sit still, I got out and walked back to the main road, where the buildings of Gaffney's place could be seen. There was, as the driver had said, a dim light, but it seemed to be in one of the rear rooms.

For five minutes all was silent. Then, far up the road, I thought I heard the beat of horses' hoofs coming on at a jog-trot. Listening intently, I soon was assured. Nothing could be seen along the dark shadow of the hedgerow; the light was too feeble to point out objects in the road; but every moment, more and more distinctly, I heard what I felt certain to be a horse and buggy coming towards us. Then all of a sudden the sound ceased.

The approach to Gaffney's was a semicircular sweep of shell road leading from the main highway to the galleries of the saloon. There was probably a distance of a hundred yards between the two entrances. I was standing at the northern end. That buggy had evidently stopped at or very near the other. I almost fancied I could see it. Now, had Parker heard it coming? Waiting a moment more in breathless expectancy, I suddenly heard, as though from the shrubbery in front of Gaffney's, low, prolonged, and clear, a whistle. My nerves leaped with sudden start. The same odd thrill of tremulous excitement seized me that had so mastered me that strange night in the old plantation home at Sandbrook. It was for all the world like the signal-whistle that had so roused me that night, only very much softer. Could it have been from Mr. Parker? Whether it was or no he would probably need me now. I crept into the shadow of the hedgerow and, on tiptoe, hastened up the curve towards the gallery. A dim figure was standing at the end of the house peering towards the other entrance,—a figure that held out a warning hand, and I stole noiselessly up beside it, my heart beating like a trip-hammer. It was Parker.

"Quiet," he whispered; "I think we have treed our buggy friends."

"The buggy is out there on the road," I answered.

"It was, but that whistle will bring it in here.

There stands the big man just at the other end of the gallery. He cannot see us; he is looking the other way. Follow me across into the shrubbery and we will get up near him. I'm bound to hear what devilment they are up to."

With that he sprang lightly across. I followed; and, crouching noiselessly along the soft grass, we stole through the low trees and bushes until nearly opposite the southern end of the gallery. Almost at the same instant the buggy came driving up the turn, and a voice uttered an impatient "Whoa!"

"What have you seen?" queried the party in the buggy in a low, agitated voice,—a voice I knew I had heard before, and instinctively reached forth my hand and placed it on my companion's arm.

"Seen! Not a d—d thing. Your blue-bellied skunk has been too smart for you, Cap. He not only hasn't come himself, but he's got his friends out here on your track."

"He has come, I tell you," answered the first speaker. "You know yourself they were asking for him at Gaston's, and that fellow at the bridge told you he saw him ride across."

"Then where'd he go to?" said the other, sulkily and savagely. "No man passed Gaston's on horseback, I can swear to that; and if he came at all as far as the bridge, why didn't he come the rest of the way? Where did he go?

How did he get back? Are you sure you wrote plain directions?"

"Plain! Of course I did. I wrote turn towards the lake, to the south, after crossing the bridge, and he'd find me; and so he would, d—n him!" added the younger man between his teeth. His voice was growing more and more familiar to me every moment in its sulky, peevish tones.

"But you said he was a stranger here. How was he to know where the lake lay?"

"Suppose he didn't! I told him to turn south. Any man knows north from south I reckon. Perhaps the white-livered sneak was a Yank at bottom, and lost his nerve."

"Tain't likely. Not from what I seen of him. His kind don't scare so d—d easy at yours, and he came out here to find you, you bet. Why didn't you say turn to the right instead of south? Damfino which is north or south here anyhow. How was he to know?"

"Don't be a fool!" said the other, impatiently, "everybody knows the river runs north and south, and Canal Street runs out right angles to the river, and you turn to the right to go to the lake. It must be south."

Here I couldn't help nudging my neighbor, the aide, who was chuckling with delight at this scientific statement.

"Well, by Gawd! you may know more 'bout

it than I do; but when I got off that boat yesterday morning up there by Julia Street, d—n me if the sun wasn't rising in the west then,—over there across Algiers,—and if the Yank is no better posted on the points of the compass than I am, strikes me he's slipped out of your trap easy enough."

"You mean he's gone to the left—past here?" asked the other, snarlingly.

"Just that. He's taken the turn to the left. None of these places this side have been open since we came out; and seeing no one, he's kept on, and probably got back to town some other way. Like enough he's in bed and asleep by this time, and here we've been fooling away the whole night."

Chilled as I was, trembling 'twixt cold and excitement, I was beginning to enjoy this conversation hugely. More than that, both the aide and myself were beginning to feel assured that Amory was safe.

"Then all we can do is go back," said the young man in the buggy, after a moment of silence. "But I'll get that fellow yet," he added, with a torrent of blasphemy. "Get in."

"Where's that flask of yours?" asked the man on the steps. "I want a drink."

"Get in first and I'll give it to you."

Then we heard the creaking of the springs, and the dim, shadowy form of the big man lumbered into the light vehicle. A gurgle and a long-drawn "ah-h-h" followed, then,—

"Got a cigar?"

"Yes; but hadn't we better wait until we get back on Canal Street before lighting them? We want to look out for those other fellows in that cab, you know."

"Oh, d—n them! You can see their lamps half a mile off. Here, give us a match."

Another minute and a feeble glare illuminated the dark interior. Pale and blue at first, it speedily gained strength and lighting power. Eagerly we scanned the two faces, now for one never-to-be-forgotten instant revealed to our gaze. One lowering, heavy-browed, coarse, and bearded; the other—ah, well I knew I had heard that voice, for there, half muffled in the heavy coat, half shrouded by the slouching hat, were the pale, clear-cut, dissipated features I had marked so keenly at Sandbrook. It was the face of Ned Peyton.

CHAPTER XIV.

ANOTHER minute the match, spluttering in the damp night air, was extinguished; but I had seen enough. To the amaze of my companion, to the scandal of any legal or professional education I might have had, indignation got the better of all discretion, and I burst through the shrubbery and laid my hand on the rein.

"Mr. Peyton, I believe," said I, in a tone intended to be double-shotted with sarcasm. "Think we had the pleasure of meeting at Judge——"

"Hell!" hissed a startled voice. "Quick,—drive on!" Crack! went the whip; the horse plunged violently forward; the wheel struck me full on the left leg and hurled me against the stout branches of some dripping bush, and with a whirr of wheels and crushing of gravel the buggy disappeared in the darkness. Mr. Parker ran to my assistance, and together we rushed to our own cab.

"Follow that buggy! Be lively!" was all I could find breath to say to our driver, and then we were off in pursuit. We heard their hoofs and wheels thundering over the bayou bridge, and saw their light vehicle flash under the lamps at the Canal Street end, and that was the last we ever did see of them. Our old horse with his heavy load was no match for theirs. Long before we reached the open road beyond the cemeteries, they were spinning along hundreds of yards out of sight ahead, and gaining at every stride. In hurried words I told the aide-de-camp who the youth was and what I knew about him, and, like myself, he was eager to overhaul him; but it was useless. Not a trace could we find of the precious pair as we drove in town. Day was breaking, and all our thoughts now turned to Amory. Where was he, and how had he escaped the trap?

In the cold, misty dawn we reined up at the Magazine Street warehouse. The sentry, with his head wrapped in the cape of his overcoat, called out the corporal of the guard, and of him we eagerly inquired. Yes. The lieutenant had returned, about an hour ago, his horse covered with mud and much "blown." The lieutenant seemed to have a chill, and had gone right to his room. Thither we followed, and noiselessly ascending the stairs, made our way out to the gallery. A dim light burned in the window; the door was half open, and by the bedside sat a soldier, who at sight of Mr. Parker rose and saluted respectfully.

"What has been the matter, orderly?" asked the aide-de-camp, in a whisper.

"I don't quite know, sir. Lieutenant Amory came home with a bad chill about an hour ago, and quick as he dismounted I came over with him, and he took some quinine and got to bed. He's just gone to sleep. He hasn't been to bed for forty-eight hours, sir, and must be used up."

We stepped forward and bent over him. He had removed his heavy riding-boots and trousers; his cavalry jacket was thrown on the chair at the foot of the bed; and, muffled up in blankets, he lay there, sleeping heavily yet uneasily. He moaned in his slumber, and threw himself restlessly on the other side as we raised the light to see his face. Placing my hand lightly on his forehead, I found it burning; so were his cheeks, his hands. Fever had certainly set in after his chill, but of how severe a character we could not judge, and it would never do to awaken him We stepped out on the landing, and after a brief consultation, decided that Parker should find the attending surgeon and send him to us as soon as possible. Meantime, I would remain with Amory.

In less than an hour the doctor arrived. Very thoroughly, yet very gently, he examined his patient as to pulse and temperature; closely scrutinized his face, and then replaced the bed-clothing that in his fevered tossing Amory had thrown off. Seeing the anxiety in my eyes, he spoke,—

"Very feverish, and probably quite ill. You did right not to wake him. He will not sleep long, and every little helps. I will stay for the present, and be with him when he does wake, for until then I cannot really judge of his condition. What a night you have had of it, Mr. Brandon! Parker has been telling me something of it."

I glanced half reproachfully at Parker. We had agreed to keep the thing to ourselves until I could see Harrod and consult with him. But the aide promptly relieved me of any misapprehension. He had "named no names," nor had he spoken of the part played by Peyton. Then, at the doctor's suggestion, we withdrew, to seek such rest as we could find after our night in the rain. Leaving Parker at headquarters, with the promise to meet him late in the afternoon, I went to my own rooms, gave my suspicious-looking landlady directions that I was not to be disturbed until noon, and, tired out, slept until after two o'clock.

When I opened my eyes, Harrod Summers rose from an easy-chair in the sitting-room, and came forward to greet me with outstretched hand. One glance at his face showed that he had something of lively interest to tell me, and as I sat up half sleepily in bed and answered his query as to whether I felt rested or any the worse for the night's adventures, I could see plainly that there was some matter that worried him, and divined quite readily that he wanted to speak with me. It all came out while I was shaving and dressing, and, dovetailed with what was already known to Mr. Parker and myself, "a very pretty quarrel" as it stood was unfolded to my ears.

It seems that on leaving the theatre the night previous, Colonel Summers had stepped ahead of Kitty and her friend, Lieutenant Turpin, and was searching for me. Seeing nothing of me in the crowd around the entrance, he looked in at one or two resorts along Canal Street, thinking it possible that he might meet some officers who could tell him of Amory's movements, and so enable him to judge of mine. Meantime, Turpin and Kitty strolled homeward, arm in arm. On reaching the Clay statue, Harrod decided to search no farther, but to go home, feeling sure that if anything were wrong I would follow him thither. At the house Pauline met him with anxious inquiry. Had he seen or heard anything of Mr. Amory? Kitty had returned ten or fifteen minutes before; had bidden Mr. Turpin a very abrupt good-night, and excused herself on the plea of fatigue and headache; and Pauline, following her to her room, found her very pale and nervous, and learned from her that Amory had been at the theatre, looking "so strangely" she thought he was ill; and, as they came down the street, two men in a buggy drove up close beside them, and leaned out and stared at them. She was utterly upset by Amory's appearance, perhaps, and thinking of him, did not notice this performance until Mr. Turpin suddenly dropped her arm and strode fiercely towards the buggy, as though to demand the meaning of the conduct of its occupants; whereupon they had whipped up and dashed off around the first corner; and one of them—though his hat and coat-collar concealed his face—one of them looked, she said, strangely like Ned Peyton. Pauline, seeing her nervousness and fright, had soothed her with arguments as to the impossibility of Peyton's being there; but she very anxiously spoke of the matter to Harrod. Then, after we had made our midnight visit, Kitty, in her loose wrapper, white as a sheet and trembling with dread and excitement, had stolen to Pauline's room. Her own window overlooked the balcony and the street, and unable to sleep, as she told Pauline, she was lying wide awake, when she heard rapid hoof-beats on the pavement coming from Canal Street,—a horse at rapid trot, but with no sound of wheels in company, and the horse halted before their door. Unable to restrain her curiosity or anxiety, she had risen, stolen to the window, and peered out through the slats of the blind. A gas-lamp threw its light upon the street in front, and there, plainly illumined by its glare, sat Frank Amory in the saddle, gazing up at her window. She turned instantly, she knew not why, and stepped back. He could not have seen her, yet, in another moment, rapidly as he came, he rode away, turned to the left at the corner, and she heard his hoof-beats dying away in the direction of Dauphin Street. That was all, until we came, and not until I had gone had she courage to creep over to Pauline and tell her what she had seen.

Early in the morning Harrod had gone to headquarters; found Amory's address, and on going thither was told by a soldier that the lieutenant was too ill to see anybody. But, on sending up his name, the doctor and Mr. Parker came down, and from them he learned that Amory had a sharp attack of fever; nothing like as serious as Vinton's, and one that would soon yield to treatment, provided nothing else went wrong. "There has been some sore trouble or anxiety which has been telling upon Amory," said the doctor, "and that complicates matters somewhat. He *may* have had some delirium last night, but not enough to cause such a freak as an all-night gallop. In fact, Parker has confided to me that Mr. Brandon and himself know something of the matter, and that they mean to have a talk with you."

"And that," said Harrod, "is what brought

me here four hours ago, though I had the grace not to disturb you. Now, what is it? What do you know? Has that young cub Peyton been at the bottom of this?"

And then I told Harrod the story of our night's adventures. He listened at first with composure; but when it came to the description of the two skulkers at Gaston's and the conversation I had overheard, he rose excitedly and began pacing rapidly up and down the room, tugging fiercely at his moustache. Every now and then some muttered anathema fell from his lips. He was evidently powerfully and unpleasantly moved, and when at last my prolix recital was brought to an end with the discovery of Peyton, and our fruitless chase, Harrod burst out into genuine imprecation,—

"The doubly damned young scoundrel!" he groaned. "Why, Brandon, I believe there is no cowardly villainy of which that fellow is not capable. I ought to have gone with you. I *knew* I ought to have gone."

"Why so?"

"Then we could have secured him by this time. It is too late now, I fear. He is off for Havana or Mexico."

"But what good would that have done? What could we prove? What would you want him secured for now that we have Amory safe and warned against him in the future? You would not care to have the thing made public, would you?"

"Not if *that* were all! By heaven! the easiest solution of the whole thing would be to let him try to trap Amory once more, and let Amory know all that—that we both know."

"Do you mean that he has been at other mischief than this mysterious attempt at Amory?"

"Yes. We thought him safely out of the way,—in Cuba. He was there, but must have come directly to this point when he heard of the verdict in those Ku-Klux cases. You know they acquitted Smith. No jury could be found that dared do otherwise, I suppose," he added gloomily.

"I knew that, of course; but why should that bring Peyton here?"

"He *had* to leave Havana, Brandon. Don't you remember father's anxiety at Sandbrook before we came away? and what he said about its perhaps being too late for any effort on his part? I was to have told you, but I couldn't bear to just yet. Why, that damned scoundrel forged father's signature to a large draft, and got the money there where the bankers knew them both. It was only discovered here in New Orleans when the draft came to the Hibernia, and as the loss comes on these old correspondents of father's in Havana, he feels bound to see them reimbursed, for he cannot bear the thought of disgrace to his name or that of a kinsman. By Peyton's arrest we might secure part of the money. That is all, for he has taken every cent father had in the world."

"Then the sooner we get to the chief of police and acquaint him with Peyton's movements and description the better it will be," said I, who felt no scruples whatever against bringing master Ned to the bar of justice.

"It's too late, Brandon, I'm afraid. He saw Amory yesterday and Kitty last night; he knows by this time we are here, and he is miles away. Father had telegraphed at once that he would refund the amount of Peyton's forged raise, and so suspended pursuit or arrest. Peyton of course has heard of this or he would not have ventured hither in the first place; but he well knows that with me here it is no place for him. We will go, of course, and start the detectives, but I fear we have lost him. Do you think Amory can see us this evening and tell us what he knows of this affair?"

"We must see him, unless the doctor prohibits it; but come first to the City Hall," said I. And as we rode thither in a street-car, both deeply engrossed in thought, Harrod turned suddenly towards me,—

"Brandon, this is the most extraordinary piece of cross-purposes to me. For three weeks— for a month past, Frank Amory has been a mystery. We all thought him growing very fond of Kitty, and after the affair on the Tennessee, where he was hurt, she seemed very much interested in him. Now for nearly a month he has avoided her, and she thinks that—well, she gave me a message for him the night we started, which virtually begged his forgiveness for something she had said or done to wound him. She would never have sent it if she did not believe he cared for her. Of course I have never delivered it, because she was here to speak for herself, and told me not to; but he has treated her with something like aversion, and she resents it, and now she's flirting with young Turpin, and then there will be more trouble. Great heavens! what a world of misunderstandings it is!" And Harrod laughed despite his anxiety.

Having some inkling by this time as to the secret of Amory's hesitancy and strange conduct towards Kitty, I told Harrod that a solution of the matter had occurred to me. There was an explanation, I believed, and a satisfactory one, and it would appear very shortly I thought. This, in profound wisdom and some mystery of manner, I imparted to the perplexed colonel. He gazed at me in bewilderment, but was polite enough to press the matter no further.

"A few days will straighten that matter," said I. "We will see when he is well enough to be about again." And in my purblind idiocy I really fancied that letter of mine to Bella Grayson was going to settle everything.

Our visit at police headquarters was brief and not particularly satisfactory. It was already past steamer time for both Havana and Vera Cruz. If Peyton were "wanted," a telegram to the quarantine station, with his full description, might establish whether or no he was on board; but there were no officers there to make the arrest, and an arrest was not wanted in any event,—it was the recovery of the money. If he had not left town it was just barely possible they might nab him; but dozens of river boats left New Orleans for a dozen different points every evening, and there were hundreds of hiding-places in the city itself. He would try, said the chief, and one or two solemn-looking men in civilian's dress came in at his call and listened attentively to our description of Peyton and his companion; but, one and all, they said they would like to hear Lieutenant Amory's account of what he had had to do with the pair. So, taking one of the detectives, we drove up to Amory's lodging.

The doctor was there and came down to meet us. I told him our dilemma, and asked if it were possible to hear Amory's story. He looked grave for a moment, and considered well before answering.

"You might see him, Mr. Brandon, if that will do. I would much rather he did not talk until to-morrow, but if there be an emergency, why, he can stand it. He is doing well, has slept well since his medicine began to take hold this morning, and now he's awake and inclined to be fretful. Something worries him, and perhaps it may be a benefit to see you."

So Harrod and the detective waited, while I went up to interview Mars.

Bless the boy's face! It brightened so at sight of me that I felt like an uncle towards him. He was very pale, rather feeble, but eagerly grasped my hand and welcomed me.

"Mr. Brandon has come to see you on business of some importance, Mr. Amory," said the doctor, "and you can talk with him, but talk as little as possible. We want to get you up and ready to travel, if you are bound to go North, so quiet will be necessary for a day or two."

With that he vanished, taking the nurse with him. Then I told Amory that Parker and I had been in search of him late at night, and fearing he was taken ill, as Vinton had been, we trailed him out to the shell road, and there came upon Peyton and a burly stranger, from whose conversation we found they were lying in wait for him. The moment they were discovered they drove off in a hurry. Could he give any clue by which we could find them? Peyton was "wanted" for a grave crime.

"What?" asked Amory, flushing, and excited.

"Forgery," I answered. "Now let me be brief as possible, Amory. I hate to excite you at such a time. Have you any idea where he is to-day, or who the other man is?"

"None whatever."

"Tell me, quietly as you can, how you came to go out there alone on horseback last night. Were you ill then?"

"Not so ill but that I knew what I was about. I had had some fever all day, probably, and—and was worried about something,—a letter from mother. She wants me to come North at once, and I would have gone but for this. Perhaps it worked on me a good deal. It was late when we got back from Jeffersonville. I wrote a note to Parker, and left it at headquarters, and went on down-town, hoping to see Vinton, and intending to dine with you at Moreau's. I did not feel well, but I wanted to see you. Right there by the City Hotel a passing cab splashed me with mud, and I turned into the barber-shop to have it rubbed off. Quite a number of men were in there, talking a good deal, and seemed to have been drinking, but I paid no particular attention to them, until just as I was leaving one of them said, 'There's the —— ——d Yank now, Peyton. What better chance do you want?' Of course I turned quickly and went right up to the fellow. One or two others sprang forward. Some one said, 'Shut up, you fool!' but it was too late.

The man was drunk, probably, and having put his foot in it, had bravado enough not to back out entirely. He was in one of the chairs, his face covered with lather, and as I inquired if he referred to me, he replied, with drunken gravity, that his friend, Mr. Peyton, had expressed a desire to meet me, and 'there he was.' Sure enough there was young Peyton, stepping out from between the chairs to his right, his face black as thunder. I was mad as a hornet, of course, and never stopped to think. 'Are you responsible for this gentleman's language?' said I. 'Just as you please,' said he; and with that I struck him full under the jaw, and knocked him back among the shaving-cups and bottles. Of course there was a terrible row. He drew his pistol, but it was yanked out of his hand by some stranger. A dozen men jumped in and separated us. I didn't know one of them, but they seemed bent on having fair play. He raved about satisfaction, and I said any time and any place. Then a gentlemanly-speaking fellow suggested that the friends or seconds meet at the Cosmopolitan, at ten o'clock; that would give plenty of time, and obviate any trouble there. And before I fully realized the situation it was agreed that we were to settle the thing according to the code, and our friends were to meet at ten o'clock. With that he was led off, and I went out to think the matter over. Of course there was nothing to do but fight. I had knocked him down and was bound to give him satisfaction. But this was no cadet fisticuff; it was a serious matter, and I needed a friend. Of course it ought to be an officer, and now that Vinton was ill, I had no one with whom to advise. I went down to the depot to find Turpin. He was a classmate, and the very fellow to back me; but Turpin wasn't there. I went to Moreau's in search of him, and—well, he was busy, and I couldn't ask him. Then I went up to headquarters for Parker. He was years ahead of me at the Point, but I knew he would see me through; but Parker was out. He lived way up-town, and when I got there they told me he had gone to the theatre. That is what brought me to the Varieties. It was getting late, and I had nobody to act for me. All those infantry fellows were strangers, and at ten o'clock I had to go to the Cosmopolitan myself. Not a soul was there whom I knew, though one or two men dropped in who looked curiously at me, and whom I thought I had seen during the row.

"It was nearly eleven o'clock, and I was well-nigh crazy with excitement and nervousness, fearing that I had made some mistake, and they could say I shirked the meeting. But just about eleven a man came in, who looked closely at me, said 'Captain Amory?' and handed me a note. There's the note, Mr. Brandon; read it."

Read it I did. It was as follows:

"LIEUTENANT F. AMORY, U.S.A.:

"SIR,—In some way for which *we* find it impossible to account, the authorities have got wind of our affair, and threatened me with arrest; but I learn from a friend that you are at the Cosmopolitan unattended. The gentlemen who were present at the time of your outrageous affront this afternoon were total strangers to me, with one exception, but I cannot believe that they have betrayed me to the police.

"As an officer you must be aware that there can be only one reparation for a blow, and, if a gentleman, you cannot refuse it. You said you would meet me any time and any place, and I hold you to your word. I demand instant satisfaction, before the police can interfere, and there is one place where, if alone, we can be sure of quiet. That is a shooting- and fencing-gallery on the shell road, where there is a room where gentlemen can settle such affairs with swords, and where every attention is paid and inviolable secrecy observed.

"Leaving my friend here with the policeman who is watching our rooms, I shall slip out by the back way and go out on horseback. If you are a man of honor you will follow. Keep on out Canal Street to the end, cross the canal on the bridge, and then turn to the south. I will watch for your horse and conduct you to the spot. The bearer of this will bring a verbal answer, all that is necessary. Reminding you once more of the outrage you have committed upon a gentleman, and of your promise to render full satisfaction at such time and place as I should demand, I am, with due respect,

"Yours, etc.,
"EDWARD HARROD PEYTON."

I read it through twice before speaking, Amory narrowly watching my face.

"And do you mean to tell me, Frank Amory, that you could be led into a snare by such a transparent piece of rascality as that?" I asked at last.

"How should I know?" said Amory, flushing. "The letter *reads* straight enough. The barbers or somebody might have told the police, and I knew only that Mr. Peyton was a relative of gentlemen and supposed him to be a gentleman. Of course I went."

"All the young scoundrel wanted was to get you there alone and unarmed, and then turn you over to that great bully he had for a terrible beating. *He* would never dare fight you fairly. This thing is a fraud on its face; no Southern gentleman would ask such a thing of a stranger as a midnight meeting without seconds in an unknown spot. Why, Amory, it is absurd, and as I tell you, and as their talk proved, he only wanted to lure you there and see you brutally pounded and mutilated. The scoundrel knew he must leave town at once, and, hating you, he wanted this low revenge first."

"Why should he hate me?" asked Amory.

"Because of your fight with those villains of Hank Smith's last December, for one thing. He was hand in glove with them all. Because of—well, another reason occurs to me that need not be spoken of just now. I ought not to let you talk so much as it is. Tell me one thing, however. You are anxious to go North, the doctor says. Can I serve you in any way?"

p

Amory hesitated. "Mother is very anxious that I should come, if possible," he faltered; "and she is right. There—there are reasons why I ought to go and settle a matter that has given me much distress. I told her of it, and she writes that only one course is open to me." And the deep dejection and trouble in his face upset me completely.

"Youngster," said I, impulsively. "Forgive me if I appear to intrude in your affairs, but you have become very near to me, if you know what I mean, in the last few months. We have learned to regard you as something more than a friend, the Summers' and I, and lately it seems to me that an inkling of your trouble has been made known to me (who *would* have said, 'I have been prying into your affairs?')—and—Frank, don't worry if it is about Bella Grayson. She is my own niece,—you may not know,—and I had a letter from her the other day."

Amory almost started up in bed (capital nurse Mr. G. S. Brandon would make for a fever patient ordinarily, you are probably thinking), but though his eyes were full of eager inquiry and astonishment, he choked back the question that seemed to rise to his lips and simply stared at me, then with flushing cheeks turned quickly away.

"I cannot explain just now; try and be content with what I tell you for a day or two," I went on. "You can hear more when you are better. One thing I want to ask you for the benefit of the detectives who are looking for Peyton. How do you suppose you were so fortunate as to escape missing him and the other blackguard? We found them just below the bridge to the right."

"I don't know," was the weary reply. "Things were all in a whirl after I got that note. I remember telling that fellow to say that I would be there without fail. Then it took some time to hurry up here and get my horse, and to write a line to mother; then I did not go straight out Canal Street. There were one or two things that had to be done; but I rode like the devil to get there, and there wasn't a soul that I could see anywhere around the far end of the bridge."

"But didn't you go down towards the lake,— to the right hand, I mean?"

"To the right? No, of course not," said Amory. "He said to the south; look at the note again and you'll find it; and I had that little compass there on my watch-chain. South was to the left, man, and,—why, it seems to me I rode all night; found myself in town and rode back to the swamps; then gave it up and came home somehow; I don't know. It was all a blur."

Then, fortunately, the doctor came back, and, with one glance at Amory's face, motioned to me that enough or more than enough had been said.

I bent over Amory and said, with the best intentions in the world of being reassuring, "Remember, do not fret about going North or about anything else of that kind; *that* is coming out all right." And with the profound conviction that it *was* coming out all right through his ministration, the recorder of this curious tangle took his leave.

CHAPTER XV.

Two days elapsed and Frank Amory failed to get better with the rapidity so slight an attack of fever should have permitted; and when it is considered that my language had been, or ought to have been, very reassuring as regarded his other troubles, there seemed to me small warrant for the doctor's ascribing his slow rally to mental perturbations. It was beginning to dawn upon me that the doctor looked upon me as something of a sick-room nuisance ever since my interview with his patient about Peyton, and that only his politeness prevented his saying that that interview had been a decided set-back. At all events, two days passed without my again seeing Mars. He was sleeping when I called, or had had a restless night, and was not to be disturbed. Yet Parker saw him twice, and brought favorable accounts; he seemed to have the luck of getting around at times when Amory was awake, and, being a cavalryman himself, the aide-de-camp had taken charge of the troop and was able to bear Amory daily bulletins of its well-doing. Vinton was rapidly improving and able to sit up a few moments each day. Pauline was radiant with hope and love; and Kitty—whom I had not seen for nearly two days, when we met again at Moreau's—Kitty once more looked pale, anxious, and wistful; I saw it the instant her eyes met mine.

Harrod told me that he had seen fit to say nothing to her of Peyton's latest escapade. It would not help matters at all and could only cause her distress. Pauline had been told in confidence, and he himself had written full particulars to the judge. The police had made no arrests or discoveries; but twice I had received visits from members of the detective force asking for further description of the burly man who was with Peyton the night of the chase. The younger man, they seemed to think, had got away to Texas, but for some reason they seemed hopeful of catching the other party, who was apparently "wanted" for something for which he could properly be held.

It was two nights after the theatre party, and once again we were dining at Moreau's; this time reinforced by Pauline and by Major Williams. It was a lovely evening in the early spring. Already the breezes from the South were freighted with the faint, sweet fragrance of the orange-blossoms; windows were thrown open, and four of us at least were placidly enjoying the spirited scene on the street below. Pauline and the major were in the midst of a pleasant chat; Harrod and I dreamily puffing at our cigars; and over on the sofa Kitty and her now absolutely enslaved Turpin were oblivious to all other objects. He, poor fellow, was bending towards her, his whole soul in his eyes, his whole heart on his lips; speaking in low tones, eagerly, impetuously. She, with feverish flush on her soft cheeks, her eyes veiled by their white lids and fringed with their sweeping lashes, was nervously toying with her gloves, yet listening, painfully listening. Harrod studied them an instant, then looked significantly at me.

"It is too bad," he said, with a shrug of his shoulders. "I suppose you see poor Turpin's woe?"

I nodded. It was hard for the boy, and Kitty was by no means blameless, but just now her conduct was the source of absolute comfort to me. In my fondness for Amory I was glad to see that now that it came to actual love-making, —now that Turpin was undoubtedly enmeshed and fluttering in her toils, the little coquette was distressed by his vehemence. She was thinking of another, and my hopes for my own young knight were high. There could be no doubt of the situation, for had we not gathered in honor of the major and his gallant young adjutant? Were we not there to break bread once more before parting,—to wish them *bon voyage* with our stirrup-cups? Their orders had come. Quiet restored to the Crescent City, Major Williams's little battalion was to return forthwith to their station in Kentucky. They were to start that night, and Turpin was facing his fate.

It was soon time to walk down "homeward," as we had learned to think of Newhall's rooms on Royal Street. Harrod and I led the way. Major Williams followed, escorting Pauline. Kitty and Turpin silently took their places in the rear, and before we had gone three squares they were out of sight behind. At the steps the major said his farewells, with many a hope that we might all meet again in our wanderings. "Say good-by to Miss Carrington for me," he added, with a smile half sad, half mischievous. "I fear poor Turpin leaves his heart here. Tell him for me to take his time; he won't be needed for an hour yet." And with a wave of his hand the soldierly fellow strode down the street.

Then, even as we stood there, Turpin and Kitty arrived. With her first glance at them Pauline's sympathetic heart seemed to realize the situation. She signalled to us to follow her, and entered at once. Unaccustomed as ever to the interpretation of feminine signals, I blunderingly stayed where I was, and Harrod hovered irresolutely in the doorway.

"Won't you come in?" we heard her say timidly, almost pleadingly, as she held out her little hand.

"No, thank you, not this time; I must catch Williams. Say good-by for me, please." He grasped her hand, and seemed to wring it hard an instant, then, pulling his cap down over his eyes, dashed away.

Kitty stood one moment looking sorrowfully after him, then slowly passed us, and went in without a word. She did not appear again that evening so long as I was there.

Early next morning a note reached me from Harrod. A telegram had just reached him from Sandbrook. "Father says he will be here to-morrow. Mrs. Amory—Frank's mother—coming on same train." And, leaving everything undone that I ought to have done at the office, I hastened up to Amory's lodgings to see what that might mean. He was sitting up, partially dressed, and would be glad to see me, said the orderly; and, stumbling up the stairs, I was shown to his room.

Very pale and rather thin looked our Mars, but his face was brighter and his eyes far clearer. He was far from strong, however, and apologized for not rising, as he held out his hand.

"Mother is coming," were almost his first words.

"So I heard. Judge Summers telegraphed Colonel Harrod that he would be here to-morrow,—at noon, I suppose,—and that Mrs. Amory was on the train. What a very pleasant surprise for all!"

"Yes. When she heard from me how ill Vinton was, and that I could not get away, the little mother must have made up her mind to come to me. It is a surprise, yet a very glad one. Where can we put her? This house is no place, and yet, it may be two or three days before I can get out, and I hate to have her alone at the St. Charles."

"Why not with the Summers' at Colonel Newhall's place? There are one or two rooms vacant, and the landlady seems very pleasant."

Mars flushed to the temples.

"I think not," he said, hesitatingly. "It—it's too far away. She would rather be up here with me, or near me. She wants so much to know Vinton, too,—has such an admiration for him; but she could not see him just now, I suppose. How is he to-day?"

"Very much better last night. So much so that Miss Summers went over and dined with us at Moreau's,—a little dinner to Major Williams and Turpin, you know," said I, soothingly, and with calm note of the twinge which seemed to shoot over Amory's features at the mention of the party. "They went back to Kentucky last night, I suppose you know," I added.

"They? No, I didn't!" said Mars, with sudden animation. "I wanted to see Turpin, too. He was here twice, but they said I wasn't well enough, or something, and he went away. Did he go back with the battalion?" he inquired, eagerly.

"Certainly. He came around to say good-by last evening."

Mars settled back in his chair with an expression of absolute relief.

Now, thought I, is the time to have a few words about Bella Grayson. It was just about time to look for the coming of her reply to my diplomatic letter, and very positively did I want to know just how matters stood between her and my cavalryman. Meddling old Polonius that I was, it seemed to me perfectly right and natural that Mars should reciprocate my warm interest in him, that he should want to tell me about Bella, and that the fact of my relationship to her should give me an added lustre in his eyes. This last, perhaps, was realized. He was more inclined to be very courteous and semi-confidential in his tone, yet he was not at ease.

It was at the tip of my tongue to make some genial, off-hand, matter-of-fact inquiry, such as "Heard from Bella, lately?" by way of putting him entirely out of all embarrassment, when, fortunately, the orderly entered, saying a gentleman asked to speak a moment with Mr. Brandon. Going out in some surprise to the landing, Mr. Brandon there encountered one of the detectives whom he had recently learned to know.

"Can you come down to the office, sir? We have one of your birds, if not both," was the extent of his communication. And dropping Amory; forgetting Bella; I went.

CHAPTER XVI.

An hour later, both Harrod Summers and myself were curiously inspecting a pair of inebriated bipeds at the police station. Both were stolidly drunk, and were plunged in the heavy sleep that resulted from their excessive potations. One, the younger, was a tolerably well-dressed youth not absolutely unlike Peyton; but all the same a total stranger. Neither of us had ever seen him before. But his companion—was Hank Smith.

The two had been guilty of some drunken turbulence in a down-town saloon, said one of the police-officers, and had attracted the attention of the "force." In the course of a wordy altercation between them a detective had dropped in, and, after a few moments' apparently indifferent lounging and listening, had suddenly gone in search of a comrade, meantime bidding the officer keep his eye on them. They were still drinking and squabbling when the detective returned. Smith was demanding payment of money which the other protested he had never received, and it was not long before the lie was given and a scuffle ensued. This was sufficient to enable the officers to arrest them as drunk and disorderly, and then to notify us. That Peyton was in some way connected with the sudden appearance of Hank Smith in the Crescent City neither of us could doubt for a minute, as Peyton's name, with many blasphemous qualifications, had been frequently mentioned in their altercation. It would be some hours before they could be in condition to account for themselves and their motives; meantime the colonel and I were devoured with impatience and curiosity. The police supposed that they had the big ruffian of our night adventure in the person of Smith, but he was not the man. His presence only added to the mystery. For several weeks after his trial at Jackson he had disappeared from our view and we had heard nothing of his movements. Now, what could have brought him here, and what connection had his wanderings with Peyton's? I vainly puzzled over this problem while studying the flushed and sodden features of this arch-reprobate. Harrod went down home again to tell Vinton of the important capture. I had to go to the office at noon, but late in the day we were again at the station, and now, still bewildered and surly, but somewhat freshened by liberal applications of cold water from the pump, the ex-leader of the Tishomingo Ku-Klux was sitting up and chewing the cud of melancholy retrospect in place of the accustomed solace of "navy plug." Very ugly and ill at ease looked Hank as the colonel quietly accosted him. He knew us both at once and seemed not at all surprised at our presence.

Our only object in intruding upon his valuable time and his placid meditations being to find out what had become of Peyton, the question arose beforehand, who should question him? Supposing that he would be disposed to conceal everything he might know, we had been planning what course to pursue; but his first remark put an end to our uncertainty.

"I'm as well as a man can be who's just over a drunk and can't get a cocktail," he growled. "Have you come to pay me that money for Cap. Peyton?" And his bloodshot eyes gleamed fiercely up at Harrod's calm features.

"How much do you claim, Smith?" was the evasive query.

"He knows d—d well. It's a round five hundred dollars, and I'll foller him to Mexico but that I'll get it out of him, if you don't pay it."

"Why did you not make him pay you yesterday?"

"Yesterday?" said Hank, starting to his feet. "He ain't got back, has he? If he's lied to me again, I'll—— Say, *is* he back?" he asked, eagerly.

"I have not seen him yet," answered Harrod,

"and I do not wish to see him. I want you to warn him never to show his face among us again. Now, supposing you are released to-night, how soon can you find him?"

"*Find* him? The young whelp! He's tricked me. He's gone to Mexico, d—n him! I came here two days ago to meet him as agreed. He was to pay me the money then, and said you was here to get it for him; and then, when I got here, he left word that he was in a scrape, and had to light out for Texas right away, and never said another word about the money, except that I might apply to him there for it ('him there' being the bedraggled-looking youth sitting up now on his wooden bench and staring stupidly about him), and—and this is what came of it, by God! The money's mine, colonel, and I earned it fairly that last scrape he was in. He swore he'd pay me if we'd help him out. They'd have jailed him sure at Holly Springs if we hadn't stood by him. It took some of the hardest swearing you ever listened to to turn that marshal off his track." And Hank's face was woe-begone as this touching reminiscence occurred to him.

"And that was the service your people rendered him, was it? You could have rendered his people a much better one by telling the truth and 'jailing him,' as you say. What had he been doing to set the marshal on his track?"

Hank looked suspiciously at me a moment.

He was apparently ready to make a clean breast of matters to Harrod, but I was one of a class he regarded with distrust. Seeing this, Harrod glanced significantly at me, and I withdrew, leaving them to work out their own conclusions.

Strolling up to headquarters and thence over to Amory's, I found him sleeping quietly and Parker reading the newspapers at his bedside. An enlivening conversation was not to be looked for in that quarter therefore, and on my speaking to Parker about a room for Mrs. Amory, who was to arrive on the following day, he replied that he had already secured one close at hand. This again left me with nothing especial to do, and in my loneliness and lack of occupation I went down to Royal Street, and came luckily upon a cheerful gathering at Newhall's, as we had learned to speak of the house wherein our Sandbrook party were quartered.

It was a still, balmy evening, and Vinton's sofa had been trundled into the sitting-room. He lay there looking rather gaunt and white, but unutterably happy, for in a low chair by his side Miss Summers was seated, and she had evidently been reading aloud before my entrance, for a little blue-and-gold volume of Tennyson lay in her lap. Harrod and Kitty were seated at the centre-table near them, and rose to greet me as I entered, but the moment she had given me her little hand, with a rather embarrassed greeting, and I went forward to Vinton's sofa, Miss Kitty dropped back to the dim light of a distant corner. I had barely time to congratulate the major on his convalescence when he inquired eagerly for Amory.

"I have just come from him," I answered. "He was sleeping quietly, and Mr. Parker was there with him. He will be all right now in a day or two. Mrs. Amory will be here to-morrow, as you doubtless know, and Parker has taken a room for her at Madame R——'s, close to headquarters."

For some moments we four sat there talking quietly about her coming and its probable benefit to Amory's health, which certainly had been suffering of late. Kitty still sat in her corner, apparently occupied with a magazine, though it was too dark to read at that distance from the lamp. Vinton, of course, was eager to hear all the particulars of the recent excitements, however, and after a few moments he asked to be fully informed.

"Yes, Brandon, tell him the whole thing. Do not spare Peyton. Do not imagine that it will shock Pauline, for I have told her all about it. Indeed, I may as well take the lead," said Harrod, "and give you briefly what Smith confessed to me to-day. It was Peyton who planned and led that ambuscade on Amory's command. He ordered his party to try and pick off Amory himself, and but for the darkness they probably would have killed him. The fellow is a scoundrel throughout, and I'm almost sorry he has escaped now. Smith says he has undoubtedly gone to Mexico, and most of the money with him. Now, Brandon, tell us your story."

There was a rustle of skirts at the other end of the room. Pauline glanced wistfully over to Kitty's corner, and I could not help looking thither myself. Without a word the little lady had risen and left the room.

Pauline rose hurriedly. "I must go to Kitty," she said. " She has been very much distressed about all this trouble of late, and she will worry herself to death." With that she, too, was gone; and Mr. Brandon, bereft of his feminine audience, told his story with far less interest and enjoyment than he would otherwise have felt. Vinton was deeply interested, however, and greatly concerned over Amory's adventure. It was some time before Miss Summers' return, and then she brought Kitty's excuses. The latter had been persuaded finally to go to bed, for she was shocked inexpressibly at hearing that Peyton had really had the hardihood to carry out the threat of that memorable day at Sandbrook. "And more than that, she is convinced that Peyton has been striving to harm Mr. Amory here in New Orleans, and I *had* to promise that she should know the whole truth. Is it so, Mr. Brandon?"

And once more Mr. Brandon had the gratification of relating that episode, and before another day poor Kitty was in possession of all the facts.

And yet when I met her the following afternoon her eyes were bright; her color heightened; her manner animated and almost gay. "So glad uncle was coming," was her explanation, and yet—she did not care to go to the station with Harrod, Pauline, and myself to meet uncle. This struck me as strange, and I ventured to urge her to accompany us.

"Oh, no! the carriage only holds four," was her reply.

"But you will make the fourth, and you know I'm not coming back. I'm going to drive Mrs. Amory up to see her boy at once. He's sitting up in state ready to welcome her, and we had some difficulty in persuading him that he must not attempt to leave the house. You see there is abundant room, little lady, so why not come?"

"Thanks, I think not; I'm not ready to drive," was her confused answer; and yet I saw that she had been out. Her hat and gloves lay there upon the table. Her costume was perfect—and so was her determination.

The carriage came and we drove off, leaving her smiling and kissing her hand gayly from the balcony above our heads. Pauline glanced back lovingly at her as we turned the corner.

"Isn't she exquisite?" she said to Harrod, whose eyes, too, were fixed upon the fairy-like little figure until 'twas hidden from our sight.

"Yes, and utterly incomprehensible. Last night she was in the depths of misery when she heard about Peyton's connection with that rascally business last December. Long after the rest of us had gone to bed, Pauline went in and told her the whole story of your night adventure and Peyton's further rascality, and, by Jove! it acted like a counter-irritant. She has been in a whirl of spirits all morning; but, Paulie, she should not rush out on the streets by herself. She was out nearly half an hour awhile ago."

"Not out of sight, Harrod. I had her in view from the balcony."

"What on earth could she find to do down on Royal Street for nearly half an hour without going out of sight?"

Pauline smiled demurely. "Merely making some purchases at the corner, I fancy."

"At the corner? Why, it's a cigar store."

"I did not say *in* the corner, *M. le colonel*. Kitty is fond of oranges."

"Then it took half an hour to buy half a dozen oranges of that old Dago at the fruit-stand, did it? Still, that does not account for her blithe spirits. One would think that having sent one adorer away heart-broken; and another having vanished in disgrace (though that *was* but a boy and girl affair), and a third laid up as the result of the second's rascality; a girl might be expected to suffer some pangs of remorse. I declare I believe some women have no more conscience than kittens, and our Kitty is one of them," said Harrod, half wrathfully.

A moment's silence, then,—

"Well, *why* should she not want to come and meet the judge?" I asked, with blundering persistency.

"And *why* should she be bright as a button this afternoon?" demanded Harrod.

Pauline smiled with conscious superiority. "I can understand it readily, and am really surprised that you two profound thinkers should be so utterly in the dark. I'm not going to betray her, however; you ought to be able to see through it yourselves." And that silenced me completely. I record it with absolute humility that not until days afterwards was it made clear to me that when Pauline told Kitty the story of Amory's night-ride, the latter was able to account for the first time for his extraordinary conduct at Moreau's and the theatre; more than that, the child then knew what it was that had brought him in the dead of night to take one look at her window before going out to meet Peyton. As for her refusal to go to the depot, she simply felt unable to meet in that way Frank Amory's mother.

The train came in on time. Harrod sprang aboard, and in another moment emerged from the Pullman escorting his gray-haired father, and with them appeared the pale, placid face I had so admired in the picture at Amory's tent. Dressed in black, though not in deep mourning, the gentle lady stepped from the car, and Miss Summers, who had extended her right hand, gave one swift glance in the peaceful eyes, then suddenly, impulsively, threw forward both; and Harrod and I had abundant time to welcome the judge before either lady had a word for us. When I turned again to look at them Mrs. Amory and Pauline were still standing hand in hand, and the latter's lovely face, flushed with happiness, and with eyes that glistened through the starting tears, was hardly more beautiful than the sweet, sorrow-worn features of her who had found "that peace which the world cannot give," and in the sanctity of her bereaved life had learned the lesson of resignation,—the blessed hope of a blessed future. We would not interrupt them as they stood gazing into each other's eyes—the mother and her boy's devoted friend. It seemed best that from Pauline she should hear of Frank's improvement; of his captain's convalescence; and that the bonds of sympathy that drew them in such close alliance should there be riveted without my customary interference; but neither lady was forgetful of us, and turning to me, Mrs. Amory, in that soft, sweet voice men love to hear,—all the more winning for its Southern accent,—asked,—

"And is not this Mr. Brandon, my boy's friend?" And then Mr. Brandon had the happiness of clasping her hand, and presently of leading her to her carriage. She was impatient to get to her son, and it was soon arranged that Pauline should drive up to see her later in the evening, and then we separated. Ten minutes more and the orderly opened the door, and, obedient to my beckoning finger, stepped out as the lady was ushered in. We only heard the glad ring in Frank's brave young voice; one cry of "Mother!" and then we closed the door and left them together.

An hour afterwards, Mr. Parker and I walked over from headquarters to pay our respects to Mrs. Amory and escort her to her lodgings, where hospitable Madame R—— was waiting to welcome her and refresh her with tea. We found the doctor there in blithe chat with his patient and that now happy mother. Very sweet and gentle was her greeting for us. She seemed to know just what to say to each and every one, and charmed Parker at once, as she had me, by her lovely manner and voice. Almost the first question was, "Can we not move Frank over with me?"

But Mars protested. Here he was right near his troop; could hear the trumpet-calls and the voices of the men at times; and so felt *with* them. The doctor would not let him go to duty for forty-eight hours at the least,—perhaps not then,—and he wanted to remain where he was.

Parker laughingly offered to come and occupy the room if he really thought an officer must be with the troop, and then the doctor said his say. A carriage could be there in ten minutes; he was all dressed; he might just as well move over to Madame's, a square away; be in comfortable quarters, and have his mother in the adjoining room. The project was decided on in spite of him. Parker scurried over to Camp Street, and came back with information that just such rooms as were needed were there in readiness, and when the carriage came, our boy was half lifted, half led, down the stairs, and correspondingly transferred to new and cosey quarters nearly opposite headquarters. Some of the men brought over the trunk and his few belongings, but when it came time to start, Mars himself had stretched forth his hand and gathered in a beautiful bunch of sweet wild violets whose fragrance had filled the little room. I had noticed them on the table by his side the moment we entered, and now conceived it time to inquire whence they came.

"I'm not quite sure," said Amory, with something vastly like a blush. "They were left here an hour or so before mother came, and I think Miss Summers must have sent them."

And yet that evening, when Pauline and Colonel Summers came to see Mrs. Amory for a few moments, I was still there. The violets were by Amory's bedside up-stairs; Mrs. Amory made no allusion to them, but I did, unblushingly; and neither affirming nor denying that she had sent them, Miss Summers silenced me by saying that she was glad they gave Mr. Amory pleasure, and instantly changed the subject and addressed her talk to her lady friend. Driving home, however, she was at my mercy and I again pressed the matter. A keen suspicion was actually beginning to glimmer in my brain.

"*You* sent those violets of course, Miss Summers?"

"If so, why ask me, Mr. Brandon?"

"Well! *Didn't* you, then?"

"No, sir; I never even knew of their being sent." And Miss Summers was plainly and mischievously enjoying my perplexity.

Leaving me at my rooms, the brother and sister continued on their homeward way and their enthusiastic chat about Mrs. Amory, which my unfeeling curiosity had broken in upon. It was quite late and my letters had been brought up from the office. First on the package was the one for which I was eagerly waiting,—the answer to my diplomatic missive to Bella Grayson.

Ignoring all others I plunged instanter into that, and was rewarded—as I deserved.

"DEAR UNCLE GEORGE," she wrote.—"It was such a treat and so rare an honor to receive a letter from your august hand, that for some time I could not believe it was intended for me at all. Indeed, to be *very* frank, the closing page rather confirmed me in that impression. You men always taunt us by saying that the gist of a woman's letter lies in the postscript (one cynical acquaintance of mine went so far as to say that it lies all the way through), and yet not until that last page was reached did I discover the object of yours. Now, Uncle Georgy, isn't that circumlocution itself? Confess.

"But you really *do* seem 'interested in young Amory,' as you call him; and his 'evident admiration for a fair young friend of yours—an heiress—commands your entire sympathy.' What a cold-blooded, mercenary avowal, *M. mon oncle!* or, do you—is it possible that you mean—you too are interested in her? No! That is hardly tenable as a supposition. There is something so disingenuous about the rest of the letter that your interest is evidently on his account. Thank you ever so much for 'having half a mind to take me into your confidence.' And now, how *can* I dispel your perplexity? With the best intentions in the world, how powerless I am!

"You believe he has some lady correspondent up North. Well, that strikes me as quite a reasonable supposition. Indeed, I have heard that most of them have; but what—what did I *ever* say to lead to such a remark as this: 'Knowing what susceptible fellows cadets are (from your own statements)'? What could I ever have said to give you such an impression? Why, Uncle George, *how* should I know whether they are susceptible or not? and how could you be so cruel as to allude to the dismal fact that I had been up there every summer for six or eight years, and am still Bella Grayson? Does *that* look as though I thought them susceptible?

"But seriously; you say that Mr. Amory has become involved in 'some entanglement there from which he would now gladly escape,' and you fancy that Mr. Amory has done me the honor to make me his confidante; but herein you are mistaken. Certainly I have never heard a word from him of an 'entanglement,' nor do I remember his being devoted to any young girl in particular. Indeed, he struck me as being rather general in his attentions, what little I saw of him. It would be a great pleasure, no doubt, 'to help him out of his boyish folly and into something worth having,' to use your own words, but indeed, Uncle George, you overrate my influence entirely.

"Nevertheless, I always liked Mr. Amory very

much, and am greatly interested in his romance. Perhaps if you were to tell me what he *said* to make you think he wanted to escape from his Northern entanglement, I might be able to recall some one of his flames to whom the remarks would be applicable. Tell me what you *know*, and then my 'thinking-cap' may be put on to some advantage. Just now I'm much in the dark, and, except very casually indeed, have not heard from Mr. Amory for quite a while (How definite!—G. S. B.), and as he never mentioned this new charmer to his 'confidante,' I am most curious to hear of her. Do tell me who she is, what she is like. Is she pretty? of course that is the first question; is she—anything, everything, in fact? Do be a good Uncle Georgy and write. We were all so glad to hear from you, but as I answered, I shall expect an answer equally prompt. So write speedily to

"Your loving niece,   BELLA."

When Mr. Brandon finally sought his bachelor pillow that night, it is regretfully recorded that he, like Dogberry, remembered that he was writ an ass.

CHAPTER XVII.

Two days after Mrs. Amory's arrival, I was seated in Madame R——'s cosey parlor. Beside me in an easy-chair, and dressed in his fatigue uniform, was Mars. On the table beside him were two bunches of violets in their respective tumblers. One fresh and fragrant, the other faded and droopy. It was late in the afternoon; Mrs. Amory had gone with Mr. Parker in search of a little fresh air and exercise, and Mars had dropped his newspaper to give me a pleasant welcome. He was a little languid and tired, he said; "had to write a long letter that morning." And here he looked very strangely at me, "but felt better now that 'twas gone." I could not but fancy that there was a constraint, a vaguely injured tone, in his quiet talk. There was a lack of the old, cordial ring in his voice, though he was every bit as courteous, even as friendly as ever. It was something that puzzled me, and I wanted to get at once at the why and wherefore, yet shrunk from questioning.

Somehow or other my psychological investigations and inquiries had not been crowned with brilliant success of late, and distrust had taken the place of the serene confidence with which I used to encounter such problems. "Mother has taken the letter to post," he said, "but will be back very soon. I expect her any moment." As we were talking there came a ring at the bell. A servant passed the doorway, and in an instant reappeared ushering two ladies, Miss Summers followed by Kitty Carrington.

"Why, Frank Amory! How glad I am to see you up again!" was the delighted exclamation of the former, as she quickly stepped forward to take his hand; "and here's Kitty," she added, with faintly tremulous tone. "We—Kitty hoped to see your mother, and they said she was here."

"Mother will be back in a moment. How do you do, Miss Carrington?" said Mars, looking around Pauline in unmistakable eagerness, and with coloring cheeks and brow, as he strove to rise and hold out his hand.

"Don't try to get up, Mr. Amory," said Kitty, timidly, half imploringly, as with downcast eyes, and cheeks far more flushed than his own, she quickly stepped to his side; just touched his hand, and then dropped back to the sofa without so much as a word or glance for miserable me. For several minutes Pauline chatted gayly, as though striving to give every one time to regain composure. Kitty sat silently by; once in a while stealing timid, startled glances around;

and listening nervously, as though for the coming footsteps of some one she dreaded to meet. Pauline watched her with furtive uneasiness, and occasionally looked imploringly at me.

To my masculine impenetrability there was only one point in the situation. Mrs. Amory had arrived here in town—a stranger. Miss Summers and Miss Carrington were not exactly old residents, but were "to the manner born," and it behooved them both to call upon the older lady. Why should there be any cause for embarrassment? Why should Kitty look ill at ease, nervous, distressed? Why should Mars be so unusually excited and flighty? What was there about the whole proceeding to upset any one's equanimity? What incomprehensible mysteries women were anyhow! Bella Grayson especially! What dolts they made men appear in trying to conform to their whims and vagaries! What a labor of Hercules it was to attempt to fathom their moods! What—— The door opened and in came Mrs. Amory and Parker. All rose to greet them, and I could see that Kitty, pale as a sheet, was trembling from head to foot.

At least I had sense enough to appreciate and admire once more the grace and tact and genuine kindliness that seemed to illumine every act and word of this gracious lady. Mrs. Amory went at once to Kitty; greeted her in the same low-toned yet cordial voice that had already become the subject of our admiring talk; then, after a brief word with each of us, had taken her seat with Kitty upon the sofa, and in five minutes had so completely won the trust and confidence of that nervous little body that her color had returned in all its brilliancy; her lovely dark eyes were sparkling with animation and interest; and though she talked but little, we could all see that she was charmed with Mrs. Amory's manner, and that she drank in every word with unflagging pleasure.

Mars, though keeping up a desultory talk with Miss Summers and Parker, managed to cast frequent glances at the pair on the sofa, and it was a comfort to watch the joy that kindled in his young eyes. Pauline seemed to divine his wish to watch them, and frequently took the load of conversation from his shoulders by absorbing the attention of the aide-de-camp and myself, and this gave him the longed-for opportunity to listen once in a while to the talk between his mother and Kitty. Once, glancing furtively towards his chair, Kitty's eyes had encountered his fixed intently upon her, whereat the color flashed again to the roots of her hair, and the long lashes and white lids dropped instantly over her betraying orbs. From that marvellous and intricate encyclopædia of family history, a Southern woman's brain, Mrs. Amory had brought forth an array of facts regarding Kitty's relatives that fairly delighted that little damsel with its interest. Somewhere in the distant past a North Carolina Ward had married a Kentucky Carrington; and while she herself had married an officer of the army, her sister had married a Ward; and so it went. Mrs. Amory could tell Kitty just where and whom her people had married from the days of Daniel Boone. The chat went blithely on, and so, when Miss Summers smilingly rose and said that it was time to go, Kitty looked startled and incredulous,—the dreaded interview had been a genuine pleasure to her. Mars arose and stood erect as the ladies were saying their adieux. Pauline was saying to Mrs. Amory that by the next day Major Vinton would hope to be able to drive out for the air, and as soon as possible would come to see her; and this left Kitty for an instant unoccupied. Her eyes would not wander in his direction, however; and after an instant's irresolute pause he stepped beside her, so that, as they turned to go, she *had* to see his outstretched hand. I wanted to see what was to follow, but Parker and I had sidled towards the door to escort the ladies to their carriage. Miss Summers caught my eyes; seemed instantly to read my vile curiosity, for, with a smile that was absolutely mischievous, she placed herself between me and Kitty, who was last to leave the room. I only saw him bend low over her hand; could not catch a word he said, and was calmly surged out into the hall with ungratified and baffled spirit. It was cruel in Pauline. She ought to have known that I was even more interested in the affair than any woman could have been.

"What do you think of Mrs. Amory?" I delicately and appropriately asked Miss Kitty as we drove down-town. She was in a revery, and not disposed to talk; and Miss Summers, who had invited me to take a seat in their carriage, had given me no opportunity of breaking in upon her meditations until this moment. Kitty started from her dream; flashed one quick glance at me, as she answered,—

"Mrs. Amory? I think she's *lovely*," then as quickly relapsed into her fit of abstraction. Evidently Mr. Brandon's well-meant interruptions were not especially welcome there; then, as we reached the house on Royal Street, Major Vinton, seated at the window, waved us (*us* indeed!) a joyous greeting, and, despite Miss Summers' most courteous invitation to come in a while, Mr. Brandon felt that he had been interloping long enough, and having thus partially come to his senses, the narrator walked dolefully away.

In the week that followed, there were almost daily visits between the ladies of the Royal and Camp Street households. Vinton had sufficiently improved to be able to drive out every day and to take very short walks, accompanied by his radiant *fiancée*. Much mysterious shopping was going on, Mrs. Amory and Kitty being occupied for some hours each bright morning in accompanying Miss Summers on her Canal Street researches. Mars had returned to duty with his troop, and almost every evening could be seen riding down to Royal Street to report to his captain how matters were progressing. I was struck by the regularity and precision with which those reports seemed to be necessary, and the absolute brevity of their rendition. Having nothing better to do, as I fancied, I was frequently there at Royal Street when Mars would come trotting down the block pavement. Each evening seemed to add to the spring and activity with which he would vault from the saddle; toss the reins to his attendant orderly, and come leaping up the steps to the second floor. "All serene" was the customary extent of his report to Vinton, who was almost invariably playing backgammon with Miss Summers at that hour; while the judge, Harrod, and I would be discussing the affairs of the day in a distant corner. This left Kitty the only unoccupied creature in the room, unless the listless interest bestowed upon the book she held in her lap could be termed occupation. What more natural, therefore, than that Mr. Amory should turn to her for conversation and entertainment on his arrival? And then Kitty had improved so in health and spirits of late. She

was so blithe and gay; humming little snatches
of song; dancing about the old house like a
sprite; striving very hard to settle down and be
demure when I came to see the judge; and never
entirely succeeding until Amory appeared, when
she was the personification of maidenly reserve
and propriety. Occasionally Mars would escort
his mother down, and then there would be a
joyous gathering, for we had all learned to love
her by this time; and as for Vinton—Miss Summers once impetuously declared that she was
with good reason becoming jealous. When *she*
came, Kitty would quit her customary post on the
sofa; take a low chair, and actually hang about
Mrs. Amory's knees; and all Mars' chances for a
tête-à-tête were gone. Nevertheless, he was losing
much of the old shyness, and apparently learning to lose himself in her society, and to be profoundly discontented when she was away; and
one lovely evening a funny thing happened.
There was to be a procession of some kind on
Canal Street,—no city in the world can compete
with New Orleans in the number and variety of
its processions,—and as the bands were playing
brilliantly over towards the St. Charles, Vinton
proposed that we should stroll thither and hear
the music. The judge offered his arm with his
old-fashioned, courtly grace to Mrs. Amory;
Vinton, of course, claimed Pauline; Harrod
and I fell back together; and Amory and Kitty

paired off both by force of circumstances and his own evident inclination. Once on the *banquette*, Amory showed a disposition to linger behind and take the rear with his sweet companion, but Miss Kit would none of it. With feminine inconsistency and coquettishness she fairly took the lead, and so it resulted that she and Amory headed instead of followed the party. Plainly Mars was a little miffed; but he bore up gallantly, and had a most unexpected and delightful revenge.

At the very first crossing, something of a crowd had gathered about the cigar store, and so it resulted for a moment that our party was brought to a stand, all in a bunch, right by the old Dago's orange counter to which Harrod had made disdainful allusion in connection with Kitty's mysterious mission of the previous week; and now, close beside the counter, there was seated a chatty old negress with a great basket before her heaped with violets: some in tiny knots, others in loose fragrant pyramids. The instant she caught sight of Kitty her face beamed with delight. She eagerly held forward her basket; Kitty struggled as though to push ahead through the throng on the narrow pavement, but all to no purpose. She could not move an inch; and there, imprisoned, the little beauty, bewildered with confusion and dismay, was forced to hear what we all heard, the half-laughing, half-reproachful appeal of the darky flower-vender.

"Ah, lady! you doan' come to me no mo' for vi'lets now de captain's up agin." And there was no help for it; one and all we burst into a peal of merry laughter; even poor Kitty, though she stamped her foot with vexation and turned away in vehement wrath. And oh! how proud, wild with delight Frank Amory looked as he bent over her and strove to make some diversion in her favor by boring a way through the crowd and hurrying her along! We could see him all the rest of the evening striving hard to make her forget that which he *never* could. But Kitty had only one feminine method of revenging herself, and that was on him. Womanlike, she was cold and distant to him all the evening;. left him at every possible opportunity to lavish attentions on anybody else,—even me; and after all Mars went home that night looking far from happy.

No sooner was he out of the house than Harrod turned to me with an expression of inspired idiocy on his face and said, "What was it you were all laughing at up there at the corner,— something about violets and captains?"

Whereat Kitty flounced indignantly out of the room, and we saw her no more that night.

But all this time not another word had I heard from Bella Grayson. In fact, not a word had I written to her. She had parried the verbal thrusts in my letter with such consummate ease and skill that it occurred to me I was no match for her in that sort of diplomacy. Now the question that was agitating my mind was, how was Mars to get out of that entanglement if it really existed? My efforts in his behalf did not seem to be rewarded with the brilliant and immediate success that such depth of tact had deserved; and, my intervention being of no avail, what could he expect?

Fancy the surprise, therefore, with which I received on the following day a visit from Mars himself. It was late in the afternoon; I was alone in the office and hard at work finishing some long neglected business, when the door opened and my young cavalryman appeared.

He shook my hand cordially; said that he had come to see me on personal business; and asked if I could give him half an hour. I gladly said yes, and, noting his heightened color and his evident embarrassment, bade him pull up a chair and talk to me as he would to an old chum. I can best give his story in nearly his own words.

"Mother says I owe it to you, Mr. Brandon, to tell you what has been on my mind so long. You have been very kind and very indulgent, and I wish I had told you my trouble long ago. I'll make it short as I can." And with many a painful blush—but with manful purpose and earnestness—Mars pushed ahead.

"I met Miss Grayson, your niece, during my first class summer at West Point, and got to admire her, as everybody else did. I got to more than admire her. She absolutely fascinated me. I don't mean that she tried to in the least,—she just couldn't help it. Before camp was half over I was just beside myself about her; couldn't be content if I didn't see her every day; take her to the hops, and devote myself generally. Every man in the class thought I was dead in love with her. Mr. Brandon, I—I did myself. I never ceased to think so—until last—until after that Ku-Klux fight at Sandbrook. I *made* her think so. She really tried to talk me out of it at first, —she did indeed. She said that it was simply a fancy that I would soon outgrow; and she never for once could be induced to say that she cared anything for me. She was always lovely and ladylike, always perfect, it seemed to me. She even went so far as to remind me that she was as old as I was, and far older in the ways of the world, and cadets especially. She never encouraged me one bit, and I just went on getting more and more in love with her all that year; used to write to her three or four times a week; dozens of letters that she only occasionally answered. Then she came up in June, and I was incessantly at her side. She might not care for me, but she did not seem to care for anybody else, and so it went on. She would not take my class ring when I begged her to that summer. She wore it a few days, but made me take it back the day we graduates went away; but I went back that summer to see her twice, and when I came away I swore that after I'd been in service a year I would return to New York to offer myself again; and we used to write to each other that winter, only her letters were not like mine. They were nice and friendly and all that,—still, I knew she had my promise. I thought she would expect me to come back. I felt engaged so far as I was concerned; then when I got wounded her letters grew far more interested, you know (Mr. Brandon nodded appreciatively); and then they began to come often; and, whether it was that she thought our life was very hazardous, or that the climate was going to be a bad thing for me, or that I would not recover rapidly there, her letters began to urge me to come North. I got two at Sandbrook—one the very day you were there at the tent—and two since we came here; and then—then I found only too surely that it was not love I felt for her; indeed, that I had grown to love—you know well enough (almost defiantly)—Miss Carrington. I felt in honor bound to carry out my promise to Miss Grayson, and to avoid—to—well, to be true to my promise in every way. But I was utterly miserable. Mother detected it in my letters, and at last I broke down and told her the truth. She said there was only one honorable course for me to pursue, and that was to write to Miss Grayson and tell her the same, tell her the whole truth; and it was an awful wrench, but I did it that day you were at the house. It came hard too, for only the day before a letter came from her full of all sorts of queer things. A little bird had whispered that, like all the rest, I had found my cadet attachment something to be forgotten with the gray coat and bell buttons. She had heard this, that, and the other thing; she would not reproach. It was only what she had predicted all along, etc., and it cut me up like blazes; but mother smiled quietly when I told her, said that I must expect to be handled without gloves, and warned me that I must look for very *just* comments on my conduct; and then somehow I decided that you had written to her about me. You said nothing to make me think so, and altogether I was in an awful stew until this morning."

"And what now?" I asked, eagerly.

"Her answer came. Brandon, she's a trump; she's a gem; and so's her letter. Mother's got it, and is writing to her herself. I'm inexpressibly humbled, but somehow or other happier than I've ever been." And the boy and I shook hands warmly, and Mr. Brandon bethought himself that that blessed Bella should have the loveliest Easter present the avuncular purse could buy.

"What did Bella say?" he asked.

"Oh! I can't quite tell you. It was all just so sweet and warm-hearted and congratulatory (though *that* is possibly premature), and just as lovely a letter as ever was written."

"And we may look for two weddings in the —th Cavalry, then?"

But Mars' features clouded. "Vinton and Miss Summers will be married next month; for Vinton says we may expect to be ordered to the plains with the coming of summer, but no such luck for me. I have precious little hope just now."

"And has Miss Carrington heard of our Bella?" I asked, mischievously.

"Good heavens! I hope not. That would be the death-blow to everything."

Yes, it struck me that *there* would be a weapon that Miss Kit would use with merciless power.

CHAPTER XVIII.

It was a gala night at the opera. The grand old house, so perfect in acoustic properties, so comfortably old-fashioned in design, so quaintly foreign in all its appointments, was filled with an audience composed of the music-loving people of New Orleans, and a sprinkling of Northern visitors still lingering amid the balmy odors of the magnolia and the orange-blossoms. Spring had come,—summer was coming. The sun was already high and warm enough to warrant the appearance of parasols by day; while, after it sank to rest, the ray-warmed breezes were welcomed through open door and casement; and in hundreds of slender hands the fan, swung and flirted with the indolent grace our Southern women have so readily learned from their Castilian sisterhood across the sea, stirred the perfumed air, and rustled soft accompaniment to the witchery of the music.

Entering that old French opera-house on Bourbon Street, one steps on foreign soil. America is left behind. French is the language of every sign, of the libretto, even of the programme. French only is or was then spoken by the employés of the house. French the orchestra, the chorus, the language of the play. French, everything but the music. The ornamentation of the house, the arrangement of the boxes, the very division of the audience was the design of foreign hands, and here, more readily than anywhere in our land, could one imagine oneself abroad.

These were days of triumph for the stockholders of the old company. The somewhat overgilded and too ornate decorations might have lost much of their freshness, the upholstery had grown worn and faded; but the orchestra and the company were admirable. Aiming at perfection and completeness in all details, the managers had kept up the old system of putting everything *thoroughly* upon the stage. Costumes and properties, though old, were accurate and appropriate; the chorus was full, admirably schooled and disciplined; and the orchestra, in the days when Calabresi's *bâton* called it into life, had no superior in the country. Instead of lavishing fortunes on some one marvellous *prima donna* and concomitant tenor, the aim of the management had been to secure excellent voices, good actors, conscientious artists, and so be sure of rendering an opera in its entirety,—every part well and suitably filled, instead of turning the grand creations of the great composers into mere concert recitations. One heard the opera in New

Orleans as he heard it nowhere else in the country, and there, and there only of all its places of public amusement, could one see in full force the culture and the refinement of the Crescent City.

It was a "full dress" night. The parquet was filled with men in the conventional black swallow-tail. The dress and second circles of open boxes, the *loges* behind them, were brilliant with the toilets of beautifully-dressed women; and in one of these latter enclosures were seated Miss Summers and Kitty, behind whom could be seen Vinton, Amory, and Harrod.

Leaving my seat in the parquet, I strolled up to their box immediately after the curtain fell upon the first act of "The Huguenots." Some forty-eight hours had passed since my meeting with Mars, and that vivid curiosity of mine was all aflame as to the later developments. Both ladies turned and gave me cordial welcome as I entered. Vinton made room for me behind Miss Summers' chair, and Harrod strolled out to see some friends.

Though both officers were in civilian evening dress, the story of Pauline's engagement was known among the few acquaintances she had in society, and her escort, a stranger to the city, was doubtless assumed to be the Yankee major. It was too soon after the war for such an alliance to be looked on with favor by those who had recently been in bitter hostility to the army blue, and the few glances or nods of recognition that passed between Miss Summers and a party of ladies in an adjoining box were constrained—even cold. To my proud-spirited friend this was a matter of little consequence. If anything, it served only the more deeply and firmly to attach her to the gallant gentleman, still pale and languid from his recent illness, who so devotedly hovered about her the entire evening. Her sweet, womanly face was full of the deepest tenderness as she leaned back to speak to him from time to time, and soon, with woman's quick intuition, observing that I was anxious to watch Kitty and Mars, she delightedly resigned herself to my abstraction and gave her undivided attention to Vinton.

Never in my brief acquaintance with her had Kitty Carrington looked so bewitchingly pretty. Never were her eyes so deep, dark, lustrous; never—I could plainly see—so dangerous. Never was her color so brilliant, never were her lips so red, her teeth so flashingly white; and never yet had I seen her when all her fascinations were so mercilessly levelled at a victim's heart, even while she herself was tormenting him to the extent of every feminine ingenuity. The situation was plain at a single glance.

Her greeting to me had been coquettishly cordial, and for a moment she looked as though she expected me to accept Mr. Amory's proffered chair at her back. But Mars had risen with so rueful a look in his eyes—something so appealing and wistful in his bearing—that I had the decency to decline; and with vast relief of manner he slid back into his seat, and the torment went on.

In low, eager tones he was murmuring to her over the back of her chair. She—with head half turned, so that one little ear, pink and shell-like, was temptingly near his lips—was listening with an air of saucy triumph to his pleadings,—whatever they were,—her long lashes sweeping down over her flushed cheeks, and her eyes, only at intervals, shooting sidelong glances at him. What he was saying I could not hear, but never saw I man so plunged in the depths of fascination. His eyes never left their adoring gaze upon her face, yet they were full of trouble, full of pleading that might have moved a heart of stone. But Kitty was merciless. At last there came a bubble of soft, silvery laughter and the mischievous inquiry,—

"And how should a lady answer? How—Miss Grayson, for instance?"

For a moment there was no word of reply. Amory sat like one in a daze. Then very slowly he drew back, and I could see that his hand was clinched and that his bright young face had paled. Alarmed at his silence, toying nervously with her fan, she strove to see his eyes, yet dared not look around. Mars slowly rose to his feet, bent calmly over her, and, though his voice trembled and his lips were very white, he spoke distinctly, even cuttingly,—

"Miss Grayson would have answered at least with courtesy and—good-night, Miss Carrington."

And before another word could be said he had quickly bowed to the rest of us and abruptly quitted the box.

Evidently she had tormented him until his quick, impulsive, boyish nature could bear it no longer,—until his spirit had taken fire at her merciless coquetry,—and then, giving her no chance to retract or relent, he had vanished in choking indignation. Kitty sat still as a statue one little minute, turning from red to white. Pauline, who had heard only Amory's sudden words of farewell, looked wonderingly up an instant, then seeing plainly that there had been a misunderstanding, and that remark or interference would only complicate matters, she wisely turned back to Vinton, and the rising of the curtain gave all an excuse to concentrate their eyes, if not their thoughts, upon the stage.

But the opera was an old story to me. Kitty was a novelty, a study of constantly varying phases, a picture I never tired of gazing at, and now she was becoming even more—a perfect fascination. Pauline glanced furtively, anxiously, at her from time to time, but I,—I most un blushingly watched and stared. She was manifestly ill at ease and grievously disquieted at the result of her coquetry. Her brilliant color had fled. Her eyes, suspiciously moistened, wandered nervously about the house, as though searching for her vanished knight, that they might flash their signal of recall. I, too, kept an eye on the parquet and the lobby, far as I could see, vaguely hoping that Mars might relent and take refuge there, when his wrath would have time to cool, and he could be within range of her fluttering summons to "come back and be forgiven." But the second act came to a close. Mars never once appeared. Vinton and Miss Summers once or twice addressed some tentative remark to Kitty, as though to bring her again into the general conversation and cover her evident distress; but monosyllabic replies and quivering lips were her only answer. I began to grow nervous, and decided to sally forth in search of my peppery hero. My ministrations had been vastly potent and diplomatic thus far, and might be again. So, with a word or two of excuse, I made my bow and strolled into the *foyer*.

One or two acquaintances detained me a few moments, but during the intermission between the acts I was able to satisfy myself that Mr. Amory was no longer in the house. Indeed, some of the officers stationed in town told me that they had seen him crossing the street just as they re-entered. Presently I met Colonel Newhall, and his first question was,—

"How is Vinton to-night?"

"Very well, apparently. Do you want to see him?"

"Not particularly. He is here, I believe. You might tell him that his sick-leave is granted. It may be welcome news to him—just now."

"Naturally: as he expects to be married next month."

"Yes. I'm glad he got the leave—when he did," said the colonel, as he turned away to speak to some friends.

Something in his manner set me to thinking. What could he mean by saying that he was glad Vinton had secured his leave of absence? Was any sudden move probable? Amory did say that it was current talk that their regiment was to be ordered to the frontier in the spring. Could it be that the order had already come?

I went back to the box. Kitty looked eagerly around as I entered, then turned back in evident disappointment. Not a word was exchanged between us until the close of the act; but for two occupants of the *loge* "The Huguenots" had lost all interest.

It was eleven o'clock and after as we reached the lodgings on our return from the opera. Mars had nowhere appeared, though Kitty's eyes sought him in the throng at the doorway, and, as we drew near the house, she looked eagerly ahead at a soldierly form in cavalry undress uniform. A corporal of the troop was lounging under the gas-light at the entrance. The moment he caught sight of our party he stepped forward and handed Vinton a letter.

There was nothing unusual about a letter arriving for Major Vinton—day or night. Orderlies came frequently to the old house on Royal Street with bulky missives for him; yet I felt a premonition in some inexplicable way that this was no ordinary communication. It was a mere note, and I thought the corporal said, " From the lieutenant, sir." Yet I knew it meant tidings of importance,—and so did others.

Miss Summers had withdrawn her hand from Vinton's arm as he took the note, and with deep anxiety in her paling face stood watching him as he opened and read it under the lamp. Kitty too had stepped forward, and, resting one little hand on the stone post at the doorway, gazed with equal intensity and a face that was paler yet than her cousin's. Harrod and I, a little behind them, were silent witnesses. Presently Vinton looked up, his eyes seeking the face he loved.

" What is it?" she asked.

" Our orders have come."

For an instant no one spoke. I could not take my eyes off Kitty, whose back was towards me, but who I could see was struggling hard for composure. Pauline instinctively put forth her hand, drawing Kitty closer to her side.

"Shall I read it?" asked Vinton, gently, looking at Pauline, after one hurried glance at Kitty. She nodded assent.

"It is from Amory," he said.

"DEAR MAJOR,—Parker has just met me. The orders are out. Regiment ordered to Dakota. Our troop goes by first boat to St. Louis. Your leave is granted, so it does not affect you; but— I'm glad to go. Parker says by 'James Howard' to-morrow night.

"Yours in haste,
"AMORY."

Without a word Kitty Carrington turned from us and hurried into the house.

"What on earth could take the regiment to Dakota?" asked Harrod, after a moment of silence.

"The Sioux have been troublesome all along the Missouri and Yellowstone of late, and this is anything but unexpected. We had a lively campaign against the Southern Cheyennes, you remember, and this promises more work of the same kind, only much farther north."

Pauline's eyes were filling with tears. I was plainly *de trop*, and had sense enough left to appreciate that fact at least. Promising to meet Vinton at headquarters in the morning, I took my departure. I had made up my mind, late as it was, to go and see Amory; and, late as it was, I found him in earnest talk with his mother.

"Can you spare me a moment?" I asked. "I have just heard the news, and if it be true you sail to-morrow night, you will be too much occupied to-morrow."

He had come to the door to admit me, and looked reluctantly back. Hearing my voice, Mrs. Amory came into the hall to greet me, and courteously as ever she asked me to enter; but I saw the traces of tears on her face, and knew that their time was precious.

"I want to have a moment's talk with this young man, Mrs. Amory. I will not take him farther than the corner, and will not keep him longer than five minutes at the utmost. Can you spare him that long?"

She smiled assent, but Mars hung back. He knew well that I was once again coming forward with some intervention, and his blood was up, his anger still aglow; but I was not to be denied. He seized his forage-cap and stepped out with me into the starlit night.

"There is no time for apologies from an old fellow like me, Amory," said I, placing a hand involuntarily on his shoulder. "Forgive me if I pain you, or am too intrusive. I heard what happened at the opera to-night. Would you be willing to tell me how she came to know anything about Bella Grayson?"

"I told Miss Carrington myself," said Mars, rather shortly; and his hands went down in his pockets, and a very set look came into his face as he kicked at a projecting ledge in the uneven pavement.

"You know how I've grown to like you, youngster, and *must* know that I can have no other impulse or excuse in thus meddling with your affairs. I'm fond of her too, Frank, and have seen enough to-night—and before—to convince me that she would give a vast deal to unsay those thoughtless words. I do not excuse her conduct; but she never for an instant could have dreamed of its effect, and it did not take the news of your order to make her repent it bitterly. I could see that plainly. Amory, *don't* go without seeing her."

Mars made no reply whatever.

"Have you told your mother of this misunderstanding?" I asked.

"Not exactly. I have told her—she saw I was cut up about something and asked—that something had been said that was very hard to bear, but that I had rather not talk of it now. I was too much hurt."

"Well. Then I must say nothing further, my boy; but if I may ask anything for the sake of the friendship I feel for you and for them, tell your mother the whole affair, and let her guide your action. Now, forgive me, and good-night. We will meet in the morning."

He pressed my hand cordially enough, but still made no reply to my request. "Thank you, Mr. Brandon; good-night," was all he said, and Mr. Brandon walked gloomily homeward. *Amantium iræ* might be easy things to settle if left to the participants, but were vastly easier to stumble into.

Clear, cloudless, lovely dawned the morrow, and long before office hours I had breakfasted and betaken myself to headquarters. Mr. Parker was there, and Amory had been at the office, but Vinton had as yet put in no appearance. My first question was as to the probable time of departure of the troop, and Parker's tidings filled me with hope. The quartermaster had been unable to secure transportation for the horses in the "Howard." The troops could not sail before the following day. Meantime, he said, there was to be a review of the small force in the city that very afternoon, and the general had expressed a desire to have a look at the cavalry once more before they started for their new and distant sphere of duty. It was his favorite arm of the service, and he hated to part with them.

By and by the general himself arrived, and

Major Vinton happening in at almost the same moment, "the chief" led the latter into his private office and held him there for over half an hour in conversation. An orderly was despatched for Mr. Amory, who was busily occupied over at the stables, and that young gentleman presently made his appearance, looking somewhat dusty and fatigued. The men were packing for the move and getting ready for their afternoon exhibition at one and the same time, he explained. Then Vinton came out, called his subaltern to one side, and gave him some instructions in his quiet way, and no sooner had he finished than Amory faced about and went out of the room like a shot. Then for the first time I had a chance to speak to Vinton and ask after the ladies.

"Very well; at least Miss Summers is, despite her natural concern at our sudden taking off——"

"Why, you are not going!" I interrupted.

"Yes," he answered. "As far as Memphis, at least. Then I shall leave the troop to Amory and make for Sandbrook, whither the judge and the ladies will start in a few days. That is," he concluded, with a smile, "unless some new freak takes Miss Kitty Carrington. That little lady is ready to tear her pretty hair out by the handful this morning. She did not come to breakfast at all, and I fancy she had an unusually sharp skirmish with Amory last night. By the way, I've got a note for him, and he's gone,—gone clear to the foot of Canal Street, too, to look at the accommodations on one of those smaller steamers,—and I was enjoined to give it to him at once."

"Give it to me; I'll take it," said I, all eagerness. "What boat will he be looking at? I'll get there in short order."

"He ought to be back here by noon," said Vinton. "It will take him not more than an hour."

But I was eager to see Mars myself. The note must be from Kitty, I argued; and so, indeed, I knew it to be, from the dainty envelope and superscription when the major drew it forth. My theory was that I could get that note to him in less than twenty minutes, and probably be the bearer of peace propositions. It was too alluring a prospect; besides, I was tired of waiting around headquarters doing nothing. Vinton saw my eagerness, smiled, gave me his consent and the note, and in half an hour I was at the levee and aboard the "Indiana." Mars had been there and gone. So much for my officiousness.

This time I took a cab, drove rapidly back to headquarters. Neither Vinton nor Amory was there. Mr. Parker said that the latter had galloped up not fifteen minutes after I left, reported that the "Indiana" could not take sixty horses, and was off again, he knew not whither. Vinton had gone to the stables. Thither I followed.

"The major has just driven off in the quartermaster's ambulance, and they're gone to look at some steamboat," said the corporal at the gate. "The lieutenant's horse is back, sir, but he's gone away too."

This was a complication. It was after twelve. The review was to come off at three. I wanted to go down and invite the ladies to drive with me to see it. But how could I face Kitty Carrington with that undelivered note? Over to Amory's house was the next venture. New despair. He and his mother had taken a street-car and gone up-town only a few minutes before I arrived. Now, what on earth could I do?

"The lieutenant's horse was to be sent to his quarters," the corporal had informed me, "at quarter before three, and the lieutenant probably would not be back at the stables again before that time."

For the next hour Mr. G. S. Brandon was as miserable a man as the city contained. No one at headquarters could tell where Amory had gone. No one knew when Vinton would be back. I fumed and fidgeted around the office some few minutes. Neither Colonel Newhall nor Mr. Parker could help me out in the least. There was no telling where to look for Amory. Vinton might be found down along the levee, but what good would that do? Twice the old general came trudging into the aide-de-camp's room, and looked at me with suspicious eyes from under his shaggy eyebrows,—my ill-concealed impatience and repeated inquiries made him irritable, or my undesired presence during business hours was a nuisance to him, perhaps; at all events, after I had for the tenth time, probably, repeated my hopeless remark of wonderment as to where that young gentleman could have gone, just as the general came promenading into the room with hands clasped behind his back and his head bent upon his breast, as we New Orleans people had grown accustomed to seeing or hearing of him, the old soldier stopped short, and, raising his head, testily exclaimed,—

"Mr. Brandon, what *is* the matter? Does that young officer owe you any money?"

"Money, sir? No, sir!" I answered, in all haste and half indignation. "By heavens! I wish that were the matter. The boot is on the other leg, general. I owe him something more than money. A letter, sir,—a letter from a young lady, and I undertook to deliver it two hours ago."

April sunshine bursting through storm-cloud could not more quickly soften and irradiate the face of nature than that wonderful smile of the old general's could lighten every lineament. Who that ever saw it could forget it? It beamed from the wrinkles around the kind old eyes. It flashed from his even teeth. It dimpled his cheeks into a thousand merry lights and shadows. It was sunshine itself, and with it all the old courtly manner instantly returned.

"I *beg* your pardon, sir. I beg *his* pardon, sir. God bless my soul, what an inexcusable blunder! A note from a young lady. That charming little friend of Major Vinton's? Here, Parker, you go. You see if you can't find him, sir. Bring him here, sir. Help Mr. Brandon any way you can, sir. God bless my soul, what a blunder!" And by this time we were all laughing too heartily for further words. My indignant and impetuous reply had virtually betrayed the situation.

My cab being still at the door I decided to hurry right down to Royal Street, notify the ladies of the coming review, and of the fact that the troop would not sail until the following day, though I felt sure Vinton had done that; then I could return to headquarters. Meantime that precious note was placed in Parker's hands.

Whirling across Canal Street, the cab was just turning into Royal when I caught sight of Miss Summers and Harrod on the banquette, and obedient to my shout the driver pulled up. They turned back to greet me. Yes, Vinton had sent word about the review and the good news that there was yet a day before they could sail. The colonel and his sister were going to attend to some business on Canal Street, and hurry back to meet him at the lodgings at half-past two; then they would all drive up to see the review near Tivoli Circle. Would I join them? Amory was to command the troop, as the doctor thought Major Vinton not yet strong enough to ride. But where was Amory? had I seen him?

All this was asked rapidly, as time was short, and almost as rapidly I learned that Kitty was at home, and Pauline's eyes plainly said waiting and anxious. I decided on driving thither at once and confessing the enormity of my sin of omission. I would find her in their kind landlady's parlor, said Miss Summers. So in I went.

In ten minutes Kitty Carrington fluttered into the parlor where I was awaiting her. No need to tell that hers had been a night of unhappiness, a day of bitter anxiety. Her sweet face was very pale and wan, her eyes red with weeping. How to break my news I did not know. She looked wonderingly, wistfully, at the solemnity of my face, gave me her hand with hardly a word of greeting, and stood by the table waiting for me to tell my errand, forgetful of the civility of asking me to be seated.

"Miss Kitty, I am in great trouble. Nearly three hours ago I volunteered to hurry down to the levee with a letter that Major Vinton had for Mr. Amory, but Mr. Amory and I missed each other, have missed each other ever since. He has gone somewhere with his mother, and yet must be back in time for the review, but I felt certain that letter ought to get to him at once. Yet you know they do not sail until to-morrow, do you not?"

Her head was averted, her slight form was quivering and trembling, her bosom heaving violently in the effort to control the sob that, despite all struggles, burst from her lips. She had been waiting for him all the morning. In another moment, for all answer, she had thrown herself upon the sofa, and was weeping in a wild passion of unrestrained misery. Poor little motherless Kit! and this was my doing.

In vain I strove to soothe her. In vain I protested that the letter would soon be in his hands, that no possible harm could come from the delay. Nay, in my eagerness and ludicrous distress I believe I knelt and strove to draw her hands away from her face. Then she hurriedly arose, rushed to the window, and leaning her arms upon the casement, and bowing her pretty head upon her hands, sobbed wildly. Good heavens! what *could* such an old idiot do? I was powerless, helpless, wretched.

Suddenly there came a springy step along the lower passage, a quick, bounding footfall on the stair, the clink of spurred heels upon the matting in the hall, and Frank Amory, with a world of sunshine in his glad young face, stood at the doorway. One glance showed him where she stood, still weeping piteously, still blind to his presence. One spring took him half across the room, one second to her side. I heard but one quick, low-toned, almost ecstatic cry.

"Kitty! darling! Forgive me!"

I saw his arms enfold her. I saw her raise her head, startled, amazed. Saw one wondering flash of light and joy in the tear-dimmed eyes, but of what happened next I have no knowledge, not even conjecture. For once in his life Mr. Brandon had the decency not to look, the sagacity to know that he was no longer needed, if indeed he ever had been, and the presence of mind to take himself off.

CHAPTER XIX.

LATER that lovely afternoon an open carriage whirled up St. Charles Street towards old Tivoli Circle. Its occupants were Miss Summers and Kitty Carrington, Colonel Summers and myself. At the Circle we were joined by another, in which were seated Mrs. Amory, Madame R——, and Major Vinton. We were late, it seems, and the review had already begun, so there was no time for conversation between the carriage-loads; but smiles and nods and waving hands conveyed cheery greeting, and Kitty's cheeks flamed; her eyes, half veiled as though in shy emotion, followed Mrs. Amory's kindly face until their carriage fell behind; then, detecting me as usual in my occupation of watching her, she colored still more vividly, and looking bravely, saucily up into my face, remarked,—

"Well, Mr. Brandon, have you nothing to say to me? Are you aware that you have not even remarked upon the beauty of the weather this afternoon?"

And this was from the girl whom, hardly two hours before, I had seen plunged in the depths of woe and dejection. Verily, there was nothing

I could say. Such alternations of smiles and tears, storm and sunshine, exceeded my comprehension; but it was not a tax upon even my poor powers of discernment to see that my little heroine was now blissfully, radiantly, joyously happy.

Suddenly our carriage slackened speed. Crowds began to appear on the sidewalks of the broad, dusty thoroughfare. We were off the pavement now, and driving along the "dirtroad" of upper St. Charles Street. I could hear a burst of martial music somewhere ahead, and presently Pauline exclaimed, "Here are the cavalry!"

Kitty, sitting on the indicated side, had said never a word. The next moment we rode past the line of troopers sitting stolidly on their horses and looking blankly into space ahead of them. Then, riding backwards as I was, I saw Kitty's soft cheek flushing redder, and happening to extend my left arm outwards at that instant, my hand almost came in contact with the nose of a tall chestnut sorrel, much to that sorrel's disgust, for he set back his ears and glanced savagely at me; but by that time, I had lost all interest in him and was gazing in amaze at his rider. For something absolutely incomprehensible, commend me to military love-making! Less than two hours ago I had bolted out of a room downtown leaving that deliciously pretty young girl opposite me sobbing in the arms of Frank

Amory, who, with all a devoted lover's tenderness, was striving to comfort her. Yet here she sat, apparently indifferent; yet there he sat on that very horse whose feelings I had outraged, and though we—no, she—was right under his eyes,— so close that she could stroke his charger's mane with her little hand,—he never so much as glanced at her. Mr. Frank Amory, as commanding officer of his troop on review, actually disdained to look at his lady-love.

"*Now* if at any time," thought I, "this little imp of coquetry will flash into flame and wither him when they meet,—perhaps flirt with me, *faute de mieux*, meantime," but to my utter amaze Miss Kitty took it as admirably as did Pauline. Each gave him one quick, demure, satisfied little look, as much as to say, "All right, Frank, I understand." They had learned their tactics already, I suppose, and I—was an inferior being, unable to appreciate the situation in the least.

The review went off all right, I also suppose. It was all a blank to me. The general and his aides rode down the line and our carriages had to get out of the way in a hurry. Then the troops marched over to Camp Street and down that thoroughfare, giving a marching salute as they passed headquarters. We sat in our vehicles on the opposite side of the street, and I simply stared when Amory lowered his sabre in sweeping, graceful salute and positively looked away from us, and at his chief. Why! up to this time I had been ready to take his part, and upbraid Kitty whenever there had been the faintest difference between them. Now, *now*, I actually wanted her to resent his conduct; and, with the unerring inconsistency of feminine nature, she did nothing of the kind. The instant the march was over, Frank Amory came trotting up beside us,—a glad, glorious light in his brave young eyes,—sprang from his saddle and to her side. The others he did not appear to see at all. His eyes were for her alone, for her in all their boyish adoration, in all their glowing pride and tenderness. Tearing off his gauntlet, he clasped her hand before a word was said, and she looked shyly, yet steadfastly, down into his transfigured face.

"I shall be down right after stables; mother will come sooner," was all he said. Then he condescended to notice the rest of us.

Right after stables indeed! Could you not even resent *that*, Kitty Carrington? Were you already so abject that a newly-won lover dare tell you that after his horses were seen to he would look after you? Are you already falling into the cavalry groove? learning that unwritten creed that puts the care of his mount as the corner-stone of a trooper's temple?

In a state of daze I drove homeward with the

ladies. Nobody talked much. Everybody was happy except my perturbed self. Pauline and Kitty sat hand in hand. We reached the lodgings, and were but a few moments in the parlor when Vinton appeared at the door ushering Mrs. Amory. Kitty was at the window arranging some flowers, but turned instantly, and, blushing like one of her own rosebuds, walked rapidly across the room, looking shyly up into the elder lady's face. How could I help seeing the moistened eye, the slightly quivering lip, when Mrs. Amory bent and, with one softly-spoken word, "dear," kissed the bonny face.

We masculines took ourselves off for a while. It was plain the women had much to talk about, and when they have, the sooner husbands, brothers, and lovers leave, the better for all concerned.

"Mr. Brandon," said the major, as we settled ourselves on the back veranda, "it looks as though your prognostication had come true. Our Sandbrook Ku-Klux affair has brought its romance with it."

"Two of them, major! Two of them! We might call them, in view of your modest estimate of army attractions, 'Miss Summers' Sacrifice' and, and——"

"Kitty's Conquest," said Harrod.

Swiftly through a tawny waste of whirling

waters a great steamer ploughs its way. From towering smoke-stacks volumes of smoke stream back along the tumbling wake and settle on the low-lying shores. Breasting the torrent, we have rushed past crowded levee, past sloop, and ship, and shallop, past steamers of every class and build, ocean cruisers, river monarchs, bayou traders, swamp prowlers. Lordly up-stream packets lead or follow; churches, domes, chimneys, cotton-presses, elevators, warehouses, give way to low, one-storied, whitewashed cottages, or deep-veranda'd frame homesteads on the one side, to flat and open plantations on the other. Eastward there is naught to span the horizon but one far-reaching level of swamp or trembling prairie. Westward, two miles back from the river-bank, bold barriers of forest, dense, dark, and impenetrable, shut off the view. In front lies the eddying, swirling, boiling bosom of the Mississippi,—the winding highway to the North,—sweeping in majestic curve through shores of shining green. Behind us, nestling along the grand arcs of its doubling bend, New Orleans and Algiers, close clinging to the mighty stream that at once threatens and cajoles. The river is master here, yet dreams not of his power.

Precious freight our steamer bears this bright and balmy eve. Proud of its strength and grace, it surges ahead, rumbling in the vast caverns of its seething furnaces, panting in the depths of its powerful lungs, straining with muscles that glory in their task, hurling aside from iron-shod beak the burdened billows of the opposing river. Black as Erebus the clouds of smoke from towering chimneys, white as snow the screaming steam-jets, deep and mellow the note of signal-bell, clear, ringing, rollicking the farewell chorus of our swarthy crew. Boom! goes the roar of saucy little field-piece in parting salutation to the sun, redly sinking through the forest to our left, and then, from the lower deck, what unaccustomed sound is that? A trumpet, a cavalry trumpet sounds the final tribute to departing day, and a moment later a young officer comes springing from below and joins our group upon the hurricane-deck.

Here enjoying the scene, the gliding rush of our gallant craft, the balmy softness of the Southern air, we are seated, an almost silent party of seven. We are Mrs. Amory, Miss Summers, and Kitty; Major Vinton, Mr. Amory, Harrod, and myself. We are fellow-passengers for the evening only. The troop, men and horses both, is billeted below, and under command of its young lieutenant goes through to St. Louis, thence up the Missouri to its new sphere of duties in the far Northwest. Vinton is a passenger as far as Memphis, where escorting Mrs. Amory, he takes the train to Washington. The rest of us, Pauline,

Kitty, Harrod, and I, go only up to Donaldsonville, where we arrive late at night, and take the local packet back to the city. In all the excitement and perturbation consequent upon the sudden departure of the troop; in all the hurry of preparation, requiring as it did the attention of both officers, there was no time for the interviews, the fond partings, the "sweet sorrows" incident to such occasions. An unusual thing occurred,—a bright idea struck Mr. Brandon. He proposed that the quartette should accompany the troop a short way up the river and there drink with them the stirrup-cup; and at last a proposition of Mr. Brandon's was regarded worthy of acceptance. So it happens that we are here together.

Evening comes on apace, and while Harrod is smoking somewhere forward, and our cavalrymen are paired off and slowly promenading the deck with the ladies of their love, Mrs. Amory and I are chatting quietly in the brilliant saloon, and we are talking of Mars. Her voice is soft and tremulous; her face is full of trust and peace; her eyes fondly follow him and the sweet, girlish form that hangs upon his arm as they stroll forward again after a few loving words with her.

"You have been a good friend to my boy, Mr. Brandon, and you will not forget him now on the distant frontier. It will be late in the fall before he can come East."

"So long as that! I had cherished some wild notion that we might have a double ceremony, when the major and Miss Summers are married."

"No. That would be too precipitate. She is very young yet; so is Frank for that matter, but he is thoroughly in earnest. It is not that I anticipate any change of feeling, but it is best for her sake there should be no undue haste. She will spend the time with Miss Summers until that wedding comes off, then visit relations in the North during the summer. Then 'Aunt Mary' will doubtless claim her. You know that as yet 'Aunt Mary' has had no intimation of what has been going on. Indeed, but for their sudden orders for the field, I doubt very much if the young people would have settled their outstanding differences. She is a lovely child at heart, and Frank has been a truthful and a devoted son,"— the dimmed eyes are filling now, and a tear starts slowly down the warm cheek,—" but he is impulsive, impetuous, quick, and sensitive, and, sweet as Kitty is, she has no little coquetry. It will not all be smiles and sunshine, 'bread and butter and kisses,' Mr. Brandon."

"Perhaps not, dear lady, perhaps not, yet I have no fear. He is true and brave and stanch as steel, and she is loving. God bless them!"

"Amen."

Late at night. The lights of Donaldsonville lie over our larboard bow. The broad river glistens in the glorious sheen of silvery light from the moon aloft. We are gathered in the captain's cabin on the texas and our glasses are filled. Moët and Chandon sparkles over the brim.

> "My charger is jangling his bridle and chain,
> The moment is nearing, dear love, we must sever,
> But pour out the wine, that thy lover may drain
> A last stirrup-cup to his true maiden ever."

Mr. Brandon has the floor, and eloquence, forensic, judicial, social, is fled. His idea is to say something stirring and appropriate, but his heart fails him. He can only stammer, "*Bon voyage*, boys, and safe and speedy return!" Then he slinks out into the shadow of the huge paddle-box, a vanquished man.

What a thundering uproar is made by the signal-whistle of these Mississippi steamers! The boat fairly quivers from stem to stern in response to the atmospheric disturbance created by the long-drawn blasts. For two minutes at least, in protracted, resounding, deep bellowing roar, that immense clarion heralds our approach to drowsy Donaldsonville. Three long-drawn blasts of equal length, and while they din upon the drum of the sensitive ear, not another sound can be heard. I clasp my hands to my head and shudderingly cling to the guards. All other sensations are deadened. Quick light footsteps approach, but I hear them not. Two young hearts are painfully beating close behind me, but I know it not. Clasping arms and quivering lips are bidding fond farewell so near that, could I but put one hand around the corner of the narrow passage-way, it would light on a cavalry shoulder-strap (the right shoulder, for the other is pre-empted), but I see it not. Not until the deafening uproar ceases with sudden jerk, am I aware of what is going on almost at my invisible elbow. I hear a long-drawn sibilant something that is not a whistle, is not a hiss, yet something like; I hear a plaintive sob; I hear a deep, manly voice, tremulous in its tenderness. And again the miserable conviction flashes over me that I'm just where I ought not to be,—am not supposed to be,—and yet cannot get out without ruining the impressive climax. Forgive me, Kitty! Forgive me, Frank! For years I've kept your secret. For years you never suspected that you were overheard. Nearly all your story was jotted down that very spring, but not this part, not this; and now that the brief chronicle is wellnigh closed,—now that "this part" is as old a story as the rest, and as the rest would be utterly incomplete without just such a finale, can you not find it in your hearts to forgive me for hearing your sweet and sad and sacred farewell? It was hard, it was bitter trial; it was so sudden, so brief. Yet my heart went out to you, gallant and faithful young soldier, when I heard these words, "Five long months at least, my darling. You *will* be true to me, as, God knows, I will be to you?"

And you, Kitty, rampant little rebel Kit, you whom I had seen all coquetry, all mischief, all tormenting, *was* it your voice, low, tremulous, fond as his own, that I heard murmur, "Yes, even if it were years."

A few moments more and four of us are standing on the wharf-boat, while the steamer, a brilliant illumination, ploughs and churns her way out into the broad moonlit stream. Pauline is waving her handkerchief to the group of three standing by the flag-staff over the stern. Kitty, leaning on my arm, trembles, but says no word. Tears still cling to the long, fringing lashes. Lovely are the humid eyes, the soft rounded cheek, the parted lips. She throws one kiss with her little white hand, and, as the gallant steamer fades away in the distance, her myriad lights blending into one meteoric blaze upon the bosom of the waters, the cousins seek each other's eyes. Pauline bends and kisses the smooth white brow and bravely drives back her own tears. Kitty leans her bonny head one moment upon the sheltering arm that is then so lovingly thrown around her, relieving mine, and lays her little hand upon her shoulder. A new ring glistens in the moonlight. Tiny crossed sabres stand boldly in relief upon the gold; beneath them a bursting shell, above them gleams the polished stone with its sculptured motto. I know it well. 'Tis Amory's class ring, and his is the proud device, "*Loyauté m'oblige.*"

THE END

↠REDUCED IN PRICE TO $1.25↞

THE COLONEL'S DAUGHTER;
OR,
WINNING HIS SPURS.
BY CAPTAIN CHARLES KING.
12mo. Extra Cloth. $1.25.

"The sketches of life in a cavalry command on the frontier are exceedingly vivid and interesting; and the element of adventure is furnished in the graphic and spirited accounts of affairs with the hostile Apaches. Captain King is to be thanked for an entertaining contribution to the slender stock of American military novels—a contribution so good that we hope that he will give us another."—*N. Y. Tribune.*

"The fertility of this field of garrison and reservation life has already attracted the attention of several writers. We took up the work of Captain King with the impression that it might be like some of these, an ephemeral production; we found it instead a charming work, worthy of achieving a permanent place in literature. We cordially congratulate Captain King on his accomplished success, for such unquestionably it is."—*Army and Navy Journal, N. Y.*

"There have been few American novels published of late years so thoroughly readable as 'The Colonel's Daughter,' which, if it be Captain King's first essay in fiction, is assuredly a most encouraging production."—*Literary World.*

"The volume is a remarkable work of fiction, and will be found entertaining and well worthy a careful reading."—*Chicago Tribune.*

"Not for many a season has there appeared before the public a novel so thoroughly captivating as 'The Colonel's Daughter.' Its fresh flavor cannot fail to please the veriest *ennuyé*, while its charming style would disarm the most fastidious critic. With that delicacy of touch peculiar to his workmanship, he draws now upon pathos, now upon humor, but never strains either quality to its utmost capacity, which distinctly proves that Captain King is a writer of signal ability, whose novel of 'The Colonel's Daughter' we hope is but the prelude to many others."—*Milwaukee Sentinel.*

"A departure into a new field in novel writing ought always to be welcomed. 'The Colonel's Daughter' is, strictly speaking, the first American military novel. It is a good one, and Captain King ought to follow up the complete success he has made with other stories of army life on the American frontier. The style of the author is unaffected, pure in tone, and elevating in moral effect."—*Wisconsin State Journal.*

Captain King has in this novel prepared for us a clear and interesting story of army incidents in the West. He is *au fait* in the art which made Sir Walter Scott a companion for old and young—the art which brings to the mind of the reader that sentient power which places us directly into communion with the imaginary characters filling their parts in a book. The military incidents are interwoven into the inspiring love episode that to the pages of this work add animation."—*Times-Democrat, New Orleans.*

"'The Colonel's Daughter; or, Winning His Spurs,' a story of military life at an Arizona post, written by Captain Charles King, U.S.A., and published by J. B. Lippincott & Co., Philadelphia, may rightfully claim to be a good novel. Its characters are strong and clear-cut; its plot original and well sustained, and the pictures of military life on the frontier, of Apache character, and of the physical features of Arizona Territory are realistic and fascinating."—*San Francisco Bulletin.*

"The outcome of the novel is just what every reader would wish. It is a splendid story, full of life and enjoyment, and will doubtless prove a great favorite."—*Iowa State Register, Des Moines.*

For Sale by all Booksellers.

Published by J B LIPPINCOTT COMPANY, Philadelphia, Pa

KITTY'S CONQUEST.

By CAPT. CHARLES KING, U.S.A.,

Author of "The Colonel's Daughter," "Marion's Faith," etc.

16mo. Extra Cloth. $1.00.

"A highly entertaining love story, the scene of which is laid in the South seven years after the war."—*New York Herald.*

"Capt. King has given us another delightful story of American life. The reputation of the author will by no means suffer through his second venture. We can heartily commend the story to all lovers of the American novel."—*Washington Capital.*

"Will take rank with its gifted author's vivid romance, 'The Colonel's Daughter,' and should become as popular. Capt. King writes fluently and felicitously, and in the novel under review there is not a tiresome page. Everything is graphic, telling, and interesting. The plot is of particular excellence."—*Philadelphia Evening Call.*

"'Kitty's Conquest,' a charming little story of love and adventure, by Charles King, U.S.A. The plot is laid in the South during the reconstruction period following the late war. The book is written in a most attractive style, and abounds in bright passages. The characters are drawn in a very pleasing manner, and the plot is handled very successfully throughout. It is altogether a pleasing addition to the library of modern fiction."—*Boston Post.*

"A bright, original, captivating story. The scene is laid in the South some twelve years ago. It is full of life from the word 'go!' and maintains its interest uninterruptedly to the end. The varying fortunes through which the hero pursues his 'military love-making' are graphically depicted, and a spice of dangerous adventure makes the story all the more readable."—*New York School Journal.*

"A bright and vivaciously-told story, whose incidents, largely founded upon fact, occurred some twelve years ago. The scene, opening in Alabama, is soon transferred to New Orleans, where the interest mainly centres, revolving round the troublous days when Kellogg and McEnery were *de facto* and *de jure* claimants of supreme power in Louisiana, when the air was filled with notes of warlike preparation and the tread of armed men. Though the *heroes* are, for the most part, United States officers, there is yet nothing but kindly courtesy and generous good-will in the tone of the story, and its delineations of Southern character and life, of Southern scenes, and the circumstances and conditions of the time. The author is Charles King, himself a United States soldier, whose story of 'The Colonel's Daughter' has been well received."—*New Orleans Times-Democrat.*

*** For sale by all Booksellers, or will be sent by mail, postage prepaid, on receipt of the price, by

J. B. LIPPINCOTT COMPANY, Publishers,

715 and 717 Market Street, Philadelphia.

"A BRILLIANT PICTURE OF GARRISON LIFE."

MARION'S FAITH.

By CAPTAIN *CHARLES KING,* U.S.A.,

Author of "The Colonel's Daughter,"
"Kitty's Conquest," etc.

12mo.   Extra cloth   -   -   -   -   -   - $1.25

"Captain King has done what the many admirers of his charming first story, 'The Colonel's Daughter,' hoped he would do,—he has written another novel of American army life. The present is in some sort a continuation of the former, many of the characters of the first story reappearing in the pages of this volume. The scenes of the story are laid in the frontier country of the West, and fights with the Cheyenne Indians afford sufficiently stirring incidents. The same bright, sparkling style and easy manner which rendered 'The Colonel's Daughter' and 'Kitty's Conquest' so popular and so delightful, characterize the present volume. It is replete with spirited, interesting, humorous, and pathetic pictures of soldier life on the frontier, and will be received with a warm welcome, not only by the large circle of readers of the author's previous works, but by all who delight in an excellent story charmingly told."—*Chicago Evening Journal.*

"The author of this novel is a gallant soldier, now on the retired list by reason of wounds received in the line of duty. The favor with which his books have been received proves that he can write as well as fight. 'Marion's Faith' is a very pleasing story, with a strong flavor of love and shoulder-straps, and military life, and cannot but charm the reader."—*National Tribune, Washington, D. C.*

"Captain King has caught the true spirit of the American novel, for he has endowed his work fully and freely with the dash, vigor, breeziness, bravery, tenderness, and truth which are recognized throughout the world as our national characteristics. Moreover, he is letting in a flood of light upon the hidden details of army life in our frontier garrisons and amid the hills of the Indian country. He is giving the public a bit of insight into the career of a United States soldier, and abundantly demonstrating that the Custers and Mileses and Crooks of to-day are not mere hired men, but soldiers as patriotic, unselfish, and daring as any of those who went down with the guns in the great civil strife. Captain King's narrative work is singularly fascinating."—*St. Louis Republican.*

"As descriptions of life at an army post, and of the vicissitudes, trials, and heroisms of army life on the plains, in what are called 'times of peace,' the two novels of Captain King are worthy of a high and permanent place in American literature. They will hereafter take rank with Cooper's novels as distinctively American works of fiction."—*Army and Navy Register, Washington, D. C.*

American Novels, No. 1.

THE DESERTER
- - AND - -
FROM THE RANKS.

By Captain Charles King, Author of "The Colonel's Daughter," "Marion's Faith," etc. Complete in one volume. Square 12mo. Extra cloth, $1.00. Paper, 50 cents.

"These two stories have a tone and an atmosphere wholly different from the commonplace novel of the day, and for that reason alone they are highly enjoyable."—*Boston Literary World.*

"The gallant captain has all a soldier's generous enthusiasm for lovely woman and the delights of a cosey, love-lit home, and his heroines are all sweet, wholesome women that do honor to his heart and pen."—*Germantown Telegraph.*

"Captain King has a quick and sentient touch, and his writing is that of one whose belief in mankind is untouched by bitterness. One reads his tales with the satisfying sense of a cheerful solution of all difficulties on the final page. It is a relief, indeed, to turn from the dismal introspection of much of our modern fiction to the fresh naturalness of such stories as these."—*New York Critic.*

"He tells his stories with so much spirit that one's interest is maintained to the end. The character studies are good and the plot cleverly developed."—*New York Book-Buyer.*

⁂ For sale by all Booksellers, or will be sent by the Publishers, post-paid, on receipt of the price.

J. B. LIPPINCOTT COMPANY,
715-717 MARKET STREET,
- - - - - PHILADELPHIA, PA. - - - - -

American Novels, No. 2.

BRUETON'S BAYOU,

By John Habberton, author of "Helen's Babies,"

- - AND - -

MISS DEFARGE,

By Frances Hodgson Burnett, author of "That Lass o' Lowrie's." Complete in one volume. Square 12mo. Extra cloth, $1.00. Paper, 50 cents.

"A good book to put in the satchel for a railway trip or ocean voyage."—*Chicago Current.*

"In every way worthy of the best of our American story-writers."—(Washington) *Public Opinion.*

"It is safe to say that no two more charming stories were ever bound in one cover than these."—*New Orleans Picayune.*

"'Brueton's Bayou' is an excellent tale, the motive of which is apparently to instil into the haughty insularity of the New York mind a realizing sense of the intellectual possibilities of the Southwest. The smug and self-satisfied young New York business-man, who is detained by the lameness of his horse at Brueton's Bayou, and there presently meets his fate in the form of a brilliant and beautiful girl of the region, has the nonsense taken out of him very thoroughly by his Southern experiences. 'Miss Defarge' is a strong study of a very resolute and self-centred young woman, who accomplishes many things by sheer force of will. But the most interesting and charming figure in it is that of Elizabeth Dysart, the blonde beauty, a kind of modernized Dudu,—'large and languishing and lazy,'—but of a sweetness of temper and general lovableness not to be surpassed."—*New York Tribune.*

⁎ For sale by all Booksellers, or will be sent by the Publishers, post-paid, on receipt of the price.

J. B. LIPPINCOTT COMPANY,

715-717 MARKET STREET,

- - - - - PHILADELPHIA, PA. - - - - -

American Novels, No. 4.

A DEMORALIZING - - MARRIAGE - -

By Edgar Fawcett, author of "Douglas Duane," "A Gentleman of Leisure," etc. Square 12mo. Extra cloth, $1.00. Paper, 50 cents.

"The plot is cleverly arranged, the action lively, the dialogue sweet, and the story bright and well sustained."—*New York Tribune.*

"Edgar Fawcett still stands at the head of society novelists, as his latest story testifies. It deals with society life in New York in a brilliant and realistic manner, and if it is at times satirical, the author has just grounds for employing this spice."—*Boston Home Journal.*

"Mr. Fawcett is admirably equipped to write of life in New York, the city of his birth (over forty years ago), of his education, and of his literary work. The characters that he presents are admirably drawn in bold, clear lines. He observes society keenly, and some of his bits of 'showing up' are delightfully done."—*Public Opinion* (Washington, D. C.).

"It is one of the latest of Mr. Fawcett's brilliant stories of New York life. One uses the term advisedly. His work has both depth and resplendence—the two qualities that produce the effect we term brilliancy, and which, when used in its full significance, signifies a great deal. Mr. Fawcett's novels reveal the 'veined humanity' of the complicated, intense life of the highly-organized society of the nineteenth century."—*Boston Traveller.*

⁎ *For sale by all Booksellers, or will be sent by the Publishers, post-paid, on receipt of the price.*

J. B. LIPPINCOTT COMPANY,

715-717 MARKET STREET,
- - - - - PHILADELPHIA, PA. - - - - -

www.ingramcontent.com/pod-product-compliance
Lightning Source LLC
Chambersburg PA
CBHW022107230426
43672CB00008B/1305